WATT POTTERY

An Identification And Value Guide

Sue and Dave Morris

COLLECTOR BOOKS

A Division of Schroeder Publishing Co., Inc.

Searching For A Publisher?

We are always looking for knowledgeable people considered experts within their fields. If you feel that there is a need for a book on your collectible subject and have a comprehensive collection, contact Collector Books.

Additional copies of this book may be ordered from:

COLLECTOR BOOKS
P.O. Box 3009
Paducah, KY 42002-3009

@ $19.95, Add $2.00 for postage and handling.

Printed by IMAGE GRAPHICS, INC., Paducah, Kentucky

Table of Contents

Acknowledgments

This book is dedicated to all who share in the passion for collecting Watt Pottery. Special thanks go to the following collectors and dealers who opened their homes to us and allowed us to photograph their collections. Without their generosity, support, and encouragement, this book would not have been possible.

Warren & Kay Chapman
Dale Epstein
Dorothy Hallin
Frances Hook
Margaret Jackson
Rick & Terri Lancaster - Olde Friends Antiques
Bob Markiewicz
Larry Martinson
Jim & Diann Moreland
Jack & Shirley Prestholt, Sr. - Antique Alley Antiques
Debbie Rees
Jim & Jan Seeck - Seeck Auctioneering
Dennis Thompson
Doug Upah
Chris Watt & family

A very special thank you to our three sons whose patience, understanding, and encouragement helped immensely in the completion of this book.

Introduction

In an attempt to preserve the lifestyles of times past, collectors of today are showing a growing interest in acquiring genuine Americana. Because of this trend, Watt pottery is fast becoming a forerunner in the field of collectibles.

One-time pottery center of the country, Crooksville, Ohio was the home of a family-owned and operated business that produced a pottery so unique and distinctive that it has become highly valued by collectors today. The potters and artists of the Watt Pottery Company took great pride in their ability to transform strictly utilitarian ware into works of art. The colorful hand-decorated patterns combined beauty with utility to give collectors that homespun country look so popular today.

The collecting of Watt Pottery is a wise investment, not only because of its special charm, but because of its rarity. Although many pieces do exist today, the pottery is relatively scarce and continues to increase in value.

Best of all, collecting Watt pottery is an enjoyable and challenging hobby. Uniqueness and variety of form and design provide something for everyone. The search is half the fun, but the discovery makes it all worthwhile.

Happy Hunting!

As every Watt collector well knows, #62 creamers are difficult to find. This beautiful and rare collection contains most examples of the designs that were painted on the cream-colored clay.

The bold colors and homespun beauty of Watt pottery will give any room that warm "country" look.

6

Some collectors search for any piece of Watt pottery they can find. This collection shows the tremendous variety available.

Rare and unique – this collection contains some of the most valuable and unusual Watt pottery existing today.

A collection of #62 creamers and #15 and #16 pitchers. Note that this collection contains both variations of Starflower in both #62 creamer and #15 pitcher.

7

The popular Dutch Tulip pattern blends well with the primitive "country" look.

The photos on this page and page 10 are some examples of the advertising which appeared on many Watt pieces. The advertising company's name and town was stamped in black ink, usually on the front or inside of the pieces. Sometimes a clever slogan was used. Many collectors search for unusual examples of advertising or items sold in a specific town or locale.

CHAPTER ONE

The History of Watt Pottery

The story of Watt pottery began long ago in a small town nestled in the wooded hills of southern Ohio. It is a tale of devoted craftsmen, creative persistence, success and tragedy.

The Watt family learned the pottery business from W.J. Watt, who founded the "Brilliant Stoneware Company" in 1886, in Rose Farm, Ohio. They made salt-glazed stoneware which was hand-turned or "thrown" on a kick wheel run by a footpedal and fired in a large kiln heated with coal. They made stoneware crocks, jars, and jugs of various sizes and shapes. Traveling salesmen would distribute the stoneware to general stores and hardware stores in Ohio, Northern Kentucky, and Indiana. This pottery company was sold in 1897.

W.J. Watt worked for his brothers-in-law at the Ransbottom Brothers Pottery in Ironspot, Ohio, from 1903 until 1921, until he bought the Globe Stoneware Company in Crooksville, Ohio. He renamed it the Watt Pottery Company and it was run by W.J. Watt, his sons (Harry & Thomas Watt), his son-in-law (C.L. Dawson), his daughter (Marion Watt), and a few other relatives.

In the early years of the Watt Pottery Company, from approximately 1922 until 1935, they manufactured stone containers — stoneware jars, jugs, dutch pots, milk pans, preserve jars, and various sizes of mixing bowls. Jars ranged in size from one gallon to twenty gallons. At the outset, the stoneware jars were thrown on a potters wheel, but later they purchased a "jar machine" that eliminated the hand-turning process. The early crocks and jugs were of imperial sizes and were transported to Canada to be sold. The jugs with cone-shaped tops were incised with a heart and the size impressed within the heart. In 1925 they started to diversify by making jardinieres, chicken waters, mixing bowls, and churns with dashers. The eight to twenty gallon jars were made on the new jar machine. In the latter part of 1926 they began marking the jars and crocks with a cobalt blue acorn stamp with the size written inside of the acorn.

Until this point, the Watt family managed to pay their bills, keep paying off their business loan, and keep all the employees working forty hours a week through a depressed post-World War I economy. However, in the 1930s and 1940s, a new trend spread across the country and the Watt Pottery Company made big changes by adapting its wares to this new age. Women of this new era were replacing their cast iron cookstoves with new porcelain self-lighting stoves. Electric refrigerators were so much more convenient than the old wood icebox that required a block of ice every few days. Magazine advertisements and radio commercials tempted these modern homemakers with devices and products that would save them both time and energy in the kitchen. It's no wonder that the Watt Pottery Company met with instant success when they introduced their new line of kitchen wares. When it was decided to begin producing ovenware, the Watts had to produce a ware that would withstand high oven temperatures. The clay they used was found right in the Crooksville area and was a deep cream color. When mixed with 15% feldspar and whiteners, the clay did not discolor after firing in the kilns. Thus began a line of lovely cream-colored beauties that are so collectible today.

To keep up with increased demand for kitchen wares, a continuous tunnel kiln was constructed which would fire the new kitchen ware at 2150° and run twenty-four hours a day. This very valuable addition to the factory allowed them to mass-produce over 15,000 pieces per day. In the mid 1930's the Watts discontinued making the stoneware jars, jugs, churns, and preserve jars. Plaster molds were designed for the new items which included bean pots, pie plates, covered casseroles, pitchers, cookie jars, salt and pepper shakers, spaghetti bowls, creamer and sugar sets, mugs, grease jars, and more. They installed a conveyor system in which the molds could be filled several times rather than once a day, as was done previously.

During the 1940's Watt ware was relatively simple in nature. They manufactured banded mixing bowls in graduated sizes. A blue and white band on cream pottery was one of the earliest color combinations. Much of the ware was undecorated, glazed in shades of brown. The Kla-Ham'rd series of the mid 1940's featured pieces dipped in brown glaze which had dimples on the outside of each piece to resemble "clay that was hammered." There were only fourteen different pieces produced and the line was dropped after only a few months due to poor sales.

The very first method of decoration on Watt pottery was in 1950 with the application of a rose-colored clay in the shape of a small flower with yellow stain in the center and small green leaves on either side of the flower. Although the trade name for this pattern was Wild Rose, collectors refer to it as Raised Pansy. Although these pieces are quite attractive, they were very time consuming to produce and the colors faded badly in the kilns. These pieces are very scarce because of the limited production.

The second attempt at applying the pansy decoration involved painting the large rose-colored pansy flower with yellow center and green leaves directly on the pottery. A stylus was used to cut the "veins" in the leaves. This method too proved to be unsuccessful as the stylus left rough edges of raised clay on the surface of the pottery. These pieces are also difficult to locate because of the limited production. They are commonly referred to by collectors as the Cut Leaf Pansy. The hand-painted pansy decoration did continue in production, however, the later pieces did not have the "cut leaf" veins. These later pieces will be referred to simply as Old Pansy. Both Cut Leaf and Old Pansy patterns usually have a narrow black band at the top or around the edge of each piece, but green and red bands were also used. The company trade name for these pieces was Rio Rose, but because the "Pansy" name is used by collectors, we will adhere to it. These are the very earliest of Watt decorated pottery and, although not as beautiful or popular as some of the later patterns, are highly desirable because of their scarcity and innovative designs.

By this time, a professional artist had been hired by the company to instruct the fifteen decorators working at five different stations. The company began purchasing prepared slip from a local supplier, which allowed more time for the creativity necessary in painting the pottery. Most Watt ware is individually hand-painted and no two painted pieces are exactly alike. Aside from its beauty, this unique feature makes Watt pottery so desirable to collectors.

During the 1950's Watt pottery sales soared while new patterns were offered each year. Dinnerware sets were produced in various colors of glaze and a pale pink, sometimes white, starflower. Although the trade names of these patterns were "Moonflower" (for black and green glaze) and "Silhouette" (for green flower on brown glaze), collectors group them all under the Starflower name. Particularly rare are the bright red and blue glazed pieces with a white starflower. Other floral patterns were used for these dinnerware sets, including a white dogwood pattern and a white daisy pattern on cream-colored clay, which are illustrated in Chapter 12, Miscellaneous Watt Ware.

The most popular Starflower variation with its deep red flower resembling a poinsettia and a yellow or green center and green leaves was introduced in 1951. We have no evidence that this variation of the Starflower was ever offered in dinnerware sets.

In 1952 the Apple Series was introduced and it continued in production for approximately ten years. Not only was this design the best-seller for the Watts, but it is the most desired by collectors today. The deep red apple and green leaves against the lovely cream background is truly a work of art. At first two green leaves surrounded the apple but, as the decorators became more confident, they added a lighter green shading to three dark green leaves. There were other variations of the Apple pattern which will be described in Chapter 4. The extremely rare Apple divided dinner plates were introduced in 1958 when a Ram Press was purchased by the company.

Several new patterns were introduced in the mid 1950's. The Tulip series included two completely different versions. The standard Tulip design boasts large graceful tulips, one royal blue leaning to the left and one deep red leaning to the right, with slender leaves on either side and between the flowers. The design would be repeated on the lids. The Dutch Tulip design (often referred to as Pennsylvania Dutch) was an artist's idealized tulip motif painted in a deep cobalt blue. The small leaves on this design were painted alternately in both deep red and green. Both the Tulip and Dutch Tulip are rapidly gaining popularity among collectors today.

A very colorful line called the Cherry series has deep red cherries hanging from a green stem on the right side, while a deep red flower with yellow center sits at the left side, separated by deep green leaves. The Tear Drop or American Red Bud series has a very simple pattern with deep red drooping buds resembling rose buds, light brown stems, and deep green leaves.

In 1955 the Rooster series was introduced. A seemingly crowing rooster outlined in black with green and red feathers is standing in the grass. This pattern is highly sought after by many collectors because of its individuality and scarcity.

Another popular pattern was the Autumn Foliage series which was introduced in 1959. It was easy to paint and, since it used only one color, it was produced quickly and sold well on the market. It has simple small brown leaves on brown stems.

The Morning Glory series was produced for a very limited time in the late 1950's and is extremely hard to find. It has been found in red flowers and green leaves on either cream or yellow background or cream-colored flowers and leaves on a light brown background.

Several other lines were put out in the late 1950's and early 1960's, some examples of which appear in Chapter 12. There is not an abundance of information on these pieces and they are difficult to locate. Examples of these patterns are the Eagle, Butterfly, Brown-Banded (introduced as "Bar-B-Q"), Woodgrain, and an assortment of multi-color ware in various embossed patterns such as basketweave and swirls. The Kathy Kale series of 1965 produced very few pieces, most in a brown color with a white dripped edging or white overspray, but some pieces have been located with an apple design. These pieces are marked "Kathy Kale" with a logo, illustrations of which are in Chapter 14. We believe these to be Watt pottery, however, no documentation has been found to date. This was the last line to be produced by the Watt Pottery Company.

The Watts manufactured many experimental lines of pottery to use in their sales promotions. Sometimes 500 to 1000 pieces of a particular pattern would be prepared as a sample for future business prospects. Salesmen for the company would take samples to brokers in New York City in hopes of selling them to large chain distributors. In instances where a pattern drew little interest, the line was dropped. This explains the very rare and unexplained patterns that sometimes appear today. Many times there will be no "correct" pattern name because of the multitude of variations. Chapter 13 is devoted to illustrating some of the more unusual and one-of-a-kind pieces of Watt pottery.

Many lines of Watt pottery were produced expressly for another company to market and these pieces will be marked with that particular company name. Pottery having the "R-F Spaghetti" mark were made for and sold by the Ravarino & Freschi Company, Inc. to be used in their spaghetti sales promotions. This explains the connotation "spaghetti plate" and "spaghetti bowl" used by many collectors. Other companies bearing their mark on Watt Pottery included Esmond, Heirloom, Orchard Ware, and Peedeeco, examples of which will appear in this book. Regardless of the mark, they are still considered Watt pottery since they are made by the Watt Pottery Company. The Esmond line is particularly popular and contains many interesting pieces and patterns not found in other lines.

The Watt Pottery Company produced kitchen ware from approximately 1935 until 1965. Most of the company's accounts were with grocery and hardware stores, gas stations, seed mills, and many major chain stores such as Woolworth's and Kroger's. The pottery was used for premiums in sales promotions. In these instances the advertising company's name was usually stamped in black ink either on the front or the inside of the piece.

By the 1960s, the company was producing over $750,000.00 per year in sales and looking toward $1,000,000.00 in sales by the end of the decade. Fifty percent of their products were distributed to New York and the New England states, twenty-five percent to the Chicago area, and most of the remainder was distributed throughout the midwestern and northeastern states through traveling salesmen. Although the bulk of distribution was to the midwestern and eastern states, Watt pottery was distributed to the southern and western states through chain stores, such as Safeway. Today many rare and beautiful pieces are being found in these areas of the country.

Tragedy struck the Watt Pottery Company on October 4, 1965, when fire completely destroyed the factory and warehouse, but the story does not end here. Despite the fact that Watt ware was never produced again, the pieces have withstood many years of service in America's kitchens. For the same reasons that Watt Pottery was so popular in the 1950s and 1960s, it has become a highly prized collectible today. Made from the earth by craftsmen who took pride in their work, Watt pottery was not only functional, but the vivid colors of each cheerful design create an air of homespun folk art that will make it a treasure for years to come.

CHAPTER TWO

Banded Watt Ware/Kitch-N-Queen Series

When the Watt Pottery Company introduced their new line of kitchen wares in the late 1930's, banded mixing bowls in graduated sizes were the first products offered. Most designs were offered in 5", 6", 7", 8", 9", 10", 12" and 14" diameters. Various colored bands appeared on the cream-colored bowls such as medium blue and white, light blue and white, green and white, brown, green and other colors. Pitchers, cookie jars, covered casseroles and pie plates were also produced with the banded design.

In 1955 the Kitch-N-Queen series was introduced. The bowls, pitchers, cookie jars, and covered casseroles were a cream color with one wide mauve band centered between two narrow turquoise bands. The bands appeared near the tops of the bowls, the centers of the pitchers and cookie jars, and around the outer edge of the lids. Some Kitch-N-Queen bowls were ribbed on the outside, but all have the same banding. The Kitch-N-Queen series is the most plentiful of all banded pieces and the bowls are fairly easy to find today.

Plate 1

(back row)
Blue/White Banded Casserole:
4½" high, 8¾" diameter
Marked "OVEN WARE WATT WARE USA"

Blue/White Banded Pitcher:
7" high, 7¾" wide
Marked "EVE-N-BAKE WATT WARE OVEN WARE USA"

(front row) Blue/White Banded Mixing Bowls:
Left - 2¾" high, 5" diameter
Marked "WATT OVEN WARE USA"

Center - 3½" high, 6" diameter
Marked "GOLD-N-BAKE WATT WARE OVEN WARE USA"

Right - 4" high, 7" diameter
Marked "GOLD-N-BAKE WATT WARE OVEN WARE USA"

Green/White Banded Bowls:
(smallest to largest)
#5 – 2¾" high, 5" diameter
Marked "WATT OVEN WARE 5 USA"

#6 – 3½" high, 6" diameter
Marked "WATT OVEN WARE 6 USA"

#7 – 4" high, 7" diameter
Marked "WATT OVEN WARE 7 USA"

#9 – 5" high, 9" diameter
Marked "WATT OVEN WARE 9 USA"

Not pictured: #8 (8" diameter)

Plate 2

White Banded Covered Casserole:
7" high, 9" diameter
Marked "EVE-N-BAKE WATT WARE OVEN
WARE USA"

Plate 3

Plate 4

White Banded Pitcher:
7" high, 7¾" wide
Marked "EVE-N-BAKE WATT
WARE OVEN WARE USA"

(front)
White Banded Bowl:
2½" high, 5" diameter
Marked "EVE-N-BAKE WATT
WARE OVEN WARE USA"

(back)
White Banded Bowl:
4½" high, 6" diameter
Marked "EVE-N-BAKE WATT
WARE OVEN WARE USA"

Plate 5

(front row)
Lt. Blue/White Banded
Pitcher: 7" high, 7¼" wide
Marked "EVE-N-BAKE
WATT WARE OVEN WARE
USA"

Lt. Blue/White Banded
Mixing Bowl: 4" high, 7"
diameter
Marked "GOLD-N-BAKE
WATT WARE OVEN WARE
USA"

(back row)
Lt. Blue/White Banded Cookie Jar: 7½" high, 7" diameter
at top
Marked "EVE-N-BAKE WATT WARE OVEN WARE USA"

Lt. Blue/White Banded Mixing Bowl: 5" high, 10" diameter
Marked "WATT OVEN WARE 10 USA"

Plate 6

#17 Kitch-N-Queen Ice-Lip Pitcher:
8" high, 8½" wide
Marked "WATT USA"

"Salesman's Sample"
Kitch-N-Queen Hourglass Salt and Pepper:
4½" high, 2½" diameter
No bottom mark
Ad states "THIS IS A SAMPLE IMPRINT FOR
THIS SIZE SPACE"

Plate 7

Kitch-N-Queen Ribbed
Mixing Bowls:
(largest to smallest)
#9 – 5" high, 9" diameter
Marked "WATT OVEN WARE 9
USA"

#8 – 4½" high, 8" diameter
Marked "WATT OVEN WARE 8
USA"

#6 – 3½" high, 6" diameter
Marked "WATT OVEN WARE 6
USA"

#5 – 2¾" high, 5" diameter
Marked "WATT OVEN WARE 5
USA"

Not pictured: #7 (7" diameter)

Plate 8

#503 Kitch-N-Queen Cookie Jar:
8¼" high, 8¼" diameter
Marked "WATT OVEN WARE 503 USA"

Plate 9

Kitch-N-Queen Mixing
Bowls:
(left)
#5 – 2½" high, 5" diameter
Marked "OVEN WARE 5
USA"

(right)
#14 – 7" high, 14" diameter
Marked "OVEN WARE 14
USA"

Note: This nesting set was
available in diameters of
5", 6", 7", 8", 9", 10", 12"
and 14".

Plate 10

CHAPTER THREE

Pansy Series

The Pansy pattern was the first attempt at hand-painted Watt pottery. Production began in the early 1950's and continued for several years. Although not the most popular pattern sought by Watt collectors, it is very colorful and interesting because of the many variations. Raised Pansy (also called "Wild Rose") was the first variation and involved the application of a rose-colored clay flower with yellow center and small green leaves on either side of the flower. Note that this flower is not painted directly on the pottery like all other Watt pieces, but rather dyed first and then applied. Very few of these pieces were produced because the color of the flower faded during firing in the kiln.

The next variation was the Cut-Leaf Pansy in which a large rose-colored flower with yellow center was painted directly on the pottery. A stylus was used to cut "veins" in the leaves which left roughness in the clay. The Watts continued the Pansy pattern without cutting the veins in the leaves. This variation is referred to as Old Pansy. Both the Cut-Leaf Pansy and Old Pansy usually have a narrow black band at the top, bottom, or around the edge of each piece. Some pieces will have narrow green and red bands, sometimes with the addition of small red swirls. Still another variation of the Pansy pattern is a large red flower with a white cross-shaped center and a single wide green band. This variation will be referred to as Cross Hatch. The Watts used the name "Rio Rose" in their trade journal advertising, but collectors use the term "Pansy" today. Pansy pieces are the very earliest of Watt decorated pottery and are highly collectible because of their scarcity.

Plate 11

*Raised Pansy French-Handled
Individual Casserole:
3¾" high, 7½" long
Marked "WATT OVEN WARE
USA"*

*Raised Pansy Pitcher:
7" high, 7¾" wide
Marked "EVE-N-BAKE WATT WARE OVEN
WARE USA"*

Plate 12

*Raised Pansy Refrigerator Pitcher
(lid missing):
3" high, 5½" wide
Marked "WATT OVEN WARE"*

Plate 13

Cut Leaf Pansy Sugar & Creamer:
Sugar – 2¾" high, 6" wide (handle to handle)
Creamer – 2¾" high, 6" wide (spout to handle)
Both pieces marked "WATT USA"

Plate 14

Cut Leaf Pansy Dutch Oven:
7" high, 10½" diameter
Marked "WATT OVEN WARE USA"

Plate 16

Plate 15

Plate 17

Cut Leaf Pansy Individual Spaghetti
Plate:
8½" diameter
Marked "WATT OVEN WARE R-F
SPAGHETTI"

Cut-Leaf Pansy Platter:
15" diameter
Marked "WATT USA"

21

Cut-Leaf Pansy Cup & Saucer:
Cup – 2½" high, 4½" diameter
Saucer – 6½" diameter
Both pieces marked "WATT
USA"

Plate 18

Cut-Leaf Pansy Pitcher:
6½" high, 6¾" wide
Marked "WATT USA"

Plate 20

Plate 19

Cut-Leaf Pansy Pie Plate:
1½" high, 9" diameter
Marked "EVE-N-BAKE WATT
OVEN WARE USA"

Plate 21

Cut-Leaf Pansy Mixing Bowls:
(left to right)
3½" high, 7" diameter
Marked "WATT OVEN WARE USA"

3¾" high, 8" diameter
Marked "WATT OVEN WARE USA"

4½" high, 9" diameter
Marked "WATT OVEN WARE USA"

Cut-Leaf Pansy Spaghetti Bowl:
3" high, 13" diameter
Marked "WATT OVEN WARE R-F
SPAGHETTI"

Plate 22

Plate 23

Cut-Leaf Pansy Stick-
Handled Casserole:
3¾" high, 7½" long
Marked "WATT OVEN
WARE USA"

23

Plate 24

Cut-Leaf Pansy Individual Serving Bowls:
Both bowls 2" high, 5½" diameter
Both bowls marked "WATT USA"

This photo depicts two variations of the Cut-Leaf pattern. The bowl on the left is a basic pansy pattern with no decorative bands, and the bowl on the right is commonly referred to as Bullseye Pansy by collectors because of the centered red and green bands.

Cut-Leaf Pansy Individual Spaghetti Bowl:
1½" high, 8" diameter
Marked "WATT OVEN WARE R-F SPAGHETTI"

Plate 26

Plate 25

Cut-Leaf Pansy Serving Bowls:
(left) – Bullseye Pattern
3" high, 15" diameter
Marked "WATT OVEN WARE USA"

(right) – Bullseye Pattern with red swirls
2½" high, 11" diameter
Marked "WATT OVEN WARE USA"

Plate 27

Cut-Leaf Pansy Individual Serving Bowl:
(Bullseye Pattern with red swirls)
2" high, 5½" diameter
Marked "WATT USA"

Cut-Leaf Pansy Plate:
(Bullseye Pattern)
7½" diameter
Marked "WATT USA"

Plate 28

Plate 29

Cut-Leaf Pansy Saucer:
(Bullseye Pattern with red swirls)
6½" diameter
Marked "WATT USA"

Cut-Leaf Pansy Platter:
(Bullseye Pattern)
15" diameter
Marked "WATT USA"

Plate 30

Cut-Leaf Pansy Snack
Set:
(Bullseye Pattern with
red swirls)
Plate – No bottom
mark
11¾" diameter

Cup – 2½" high, 4½"
diameter
Marked "WATT USA"

Plate 31

(left)
#2/48 Old Pansy
Casserole:
4¼" high, 7½" diameter
Marked "OVEN WARE
2/48 USA"

(right)
Cut-Leaf Pansy Casserole:
4½" high, 8¾" diameter
Marked "WATT OVEN WARE USA"

Plate 32

Plate 33

#3/19 Old Pansy Casserole:
5" high, 9" diameter
Marked "3/19 OVEN WARE USA"

Plate 34

#8 Old Pansy Four-Handled Casserole:
4¾" high, 9½" diameter
Marked "OVEN WARE R-F SPAGHETTI 8"

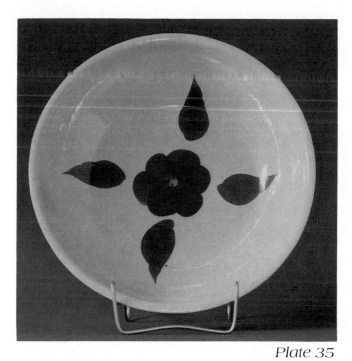

Plate 35

Plate 36

#39 Old Pansy Spaghetti Bowl:
(No black band)
3" high, 13" diameter
Marked "39 USA"

Upper Right Photo:
#39 Old Pansy Spaghetti Bowl:
3" high, 13" diameter
Marked "OVEN WARE 39 USA"

Plate 38

Plate 37

Old Pansy Individual Spaghetti Bowls:
1½" high, 8" diameter
Marked "WATT OVEN WARE R-F SPAGHETTI"

#49 Old Pansy Platter:
12" diameter
Marked "WATT 49 USA"

27

Plate 39

#31 Old Pansy Platter:
15" diameter
Marked "31 USA"

Plate 40

#15 Old Pansy Pitcher:
5½" high, 5¾" diameter
Marked "WATT OVEN WARE
15 USA"

#17 Old Pansy Pitcher:
8" high, 8½" wide
Marked "WATT 17 USA"

Plate 41

Old Pansy Pitcher:
(Cross-Hatch Pansy Pattern)
7" high, 7¾" wide
Marked "EVE-N-BAKE WATT
WARE OVEN WARE USA"

Plate 42

Plate 43

Old Pansy Cookie Jar:
(Cross-Hatch Pansy Pattern)
7½" high, 7" diameter at top
Marked "EVE-N-BAKE WATT
WARE OVEN WARE USA"

Old Pansy Spaghetti Bowl:
(Cross-Hatch Pansy Pattern)
3" high, 13" diameter
Marked "OVEN WARE USA"

Plate 45

Plate 44

Old Pansy Platter:
(Cross-Hatch Pansy Pattern)
15" diameter
Marked "WATT USA"

CHAPTER FOUR

Apple Series

In 1952 the popular "Apple" pattern was introduced and continued in production for approximately ten years. It was not only the best seller for the Watts, but it is the most sought-after pattern of Watt collectors today.

There are a few variations of the apple pattern. Earlier pieces have the deep red apple surrounded by two green leaves, but most pieces have three leaves that are shaded a light to dark green. Other variations include Reduced Decoration Apple in which the apple looks like a red heart, the Open Apple showing the apple's core, and Double Apple, with two apples instead of one. These variations which are pictured on the following three pages, are very difficult to find.

Two-Leaf Apple Pattern

Three-Leaf Apple Pattern

Reduced Decoration Apple Pattern

Open Apple Pattern

32

Double Apple Pattern

In the years that the Apple pattern was produced, many different molds were used to make a variety of kitchen ware. Because of their heavy household use, relatively few pieces exist today. Pieces such as the #15 pitcher, #33 pie plate, the salt and pepper sets, and the mixing bowls were produced in higher numbers because they were ordered by various grocery and hardware stores as premiums in their sales promotions. Pieces produced for this purpose will have the company's name and town, and sometimes an advertising slogan, stamped in black ink on the front or inside of the piece. Today's rare pieces such as the coffee pot, teapot, and oil and vinegar sets were not popular as giveaway items and were not as heavily produced. Although by no means a complete listing, this chapter will acquaint the collector with the wide variety of the beautiful Apple-patterned Watt ware. Many pieces are easily found, a few are extremely scarce — but, regardless of value, these colorful, hand-painted treasures are hard to resist.

Plate 46

#98 Apple Covered Sugar:
4½" high, 5" wide, 3¼"
diameter at opening
Marked "98 USA"
Note: Because the lids on
Watt sugars were offered as
an option, many were sold
without them.

#62 Apple Creamer:
4¼" high, 4½" wide
Marked "62"

These are the three styles
of salt and pepper sets
that Watt offered. These
pieces were not marked
because of the opening
on the bottom.
(left to right):

Apple Hourglass S/P:
(Raised letters on front)
4½" high, 2½" diameter

Apple Barrel-Shaped S/P:
4" high, 2½" diameter

Apple Hourglass S/P:
(holes on top depict "S" and "P")
4½" high, 2½" diameter

Plate 47

#56 Apple Tumbler:
4½" high, 4" diameter at top
Marked "56 USA"
Extremely Rare

Plate 48

This photo shows the four different styles of apple mugs (left to right): #121, #61, #701, #501

Plate 49

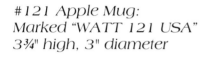

#121 Apple Mug:
Marked "WATT 121 USA"
3¾" high, 3" diameter

Plate 50

#61 Apple Mug:
Marked "61"
3" high, 3¼" diameter
Rare

Plate 51

#701 Apple Mug:
3¾" high, 3½" diameter
Marked "701 USA"
Rare

Plate 52

#501 Apple Mug:
4½" high, 2¾" diameter
Marked "WATT 501 USA"
Rare

Plate 53

Plate 54

Apple Dinner Plate:
(There are two sizes of
Apple Dinner Plates, as
follows)

9½" diameter
No mark on bottom

10" diameter
Marked "WATT USA 101"
Both Rare

36

#31 Apple Platter:
15" diameter
Marked "31 USA"

#49 Apple Platter:
12" diameter
Marked "WATT USA 49"

Plate 55

Plate 56

(left to right)
#62 Apple Creamer:
4¼" high, 4½" wide
Marked "62"

#15 Apple Pitcher:
5½" high, 5¾" wide
Marked "OVEN WARE 15 USA"

#16 Apple Pitcher:
6½" high, 6¾" wide
Marked "16 USA"

#17 Apple Pitcher:
8" high, 8½" wide
Marked "17 USA"

This photo compares the tiny Apple creamer to the various pitchers that Watt offered.

Plate 57

These are the three styles of large Apple pitchers.

(left to right)
#17 Apple Pitcher:
(no ice lip)
8" high, 8½" wide,
Marked "17 USA"

#17 Apple
Ice-Lip Pitcher:
8" high, 8½" wide,
Marked "17 USA"

#69 Apple Refrigerator
Pitcher (square shaped):
8" high, 8½" wide,
Marked "69 USA"
Rare

The plates in these two photographs are a good example of the variation in painting techniques of Watt artists. Although from the same mold, they certainly have a different appearance.

Plate 58

Apple Divided Plate:
(large shaded leaves)
10½" diameter
No bottom mark
Extremely rare

Plate 59

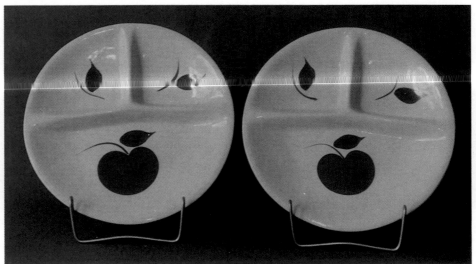

Apple Divided Plate:
(small leaves)
10½" diameter
No bottom mark
Extremely rare

Apple Tea Set: Plate 60

#505 Apple Teapot: Apple Sugar:
5¾" high, 9" wide   2¾" high, 5" wide (handle to handle)
Marked "WATT OVEN WARE   Marked "WATT"
505 MADE IN USA"
                                      All extremely rare
Apple Creamer:
2¾" high, 5" wide (spout to handle)
Marked "WATT"

                                                  Plate 61

#112 Apple Teapot:
6" high, 9" wide
Marked "WATT ORCHARD
WARE 112 USA"
Extremely rare

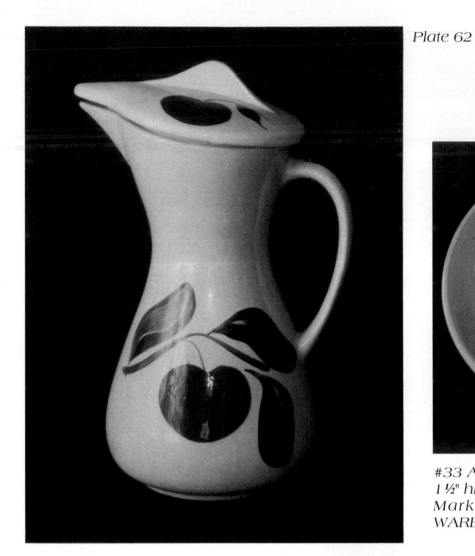

Plate 62

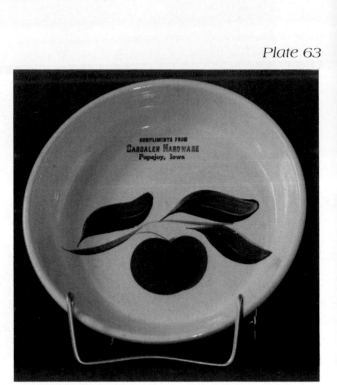

Plate 63

#33 Apple Pie Plate:
1½" high, 9" diameter
Marked "EVE-N-BAKE OVEN
WARE 33 USA"

#115 Apple Coffee Pot:
9¾" high, 7" wide
Marked "WATT ORCHARD WARE
115 USA"
Extremely rare

#126 Apple Oil/Vinegar Set:
7" high
Marked "126 USA"
Extremely rare

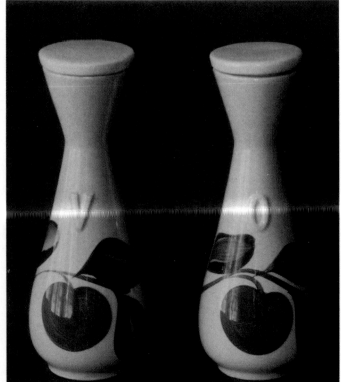

Plate 64

Apple Rectangular Baking Dish:
10" long (handle to handle)
5¼" wide, 2¼" high
No bottom mark
Extremely rare

Plate 65

Plate 66

#52 Apple Cereal/Salad Bowl:
2¼" high, 6½" diameter
Marked, "OVEN WARE 52 USA"

Plate 67

#94 Apple Cereal/Salad Bowls:
1¾" high, 6" diameter
Marked "WATT OVEN WARE 94 USA"

41

Plate 68

#74 Apple Cereal/Salad Bowl:
2" high, 5½" diameter
Marked "OVEN WARE 74 USA"

Apple Cereal/Salad Bowl:
(apple on inside of bowl only)
1 ½" high, 5¾" diameter
Marked "WATT USA"

Plate 70

Plate 69

#44 Apple Individual Spaghetti Bowl:
1 ½" high, 8" diameter
Marked "OVEN WARE R-F SPAGHETTI
44"

42

Plate 71

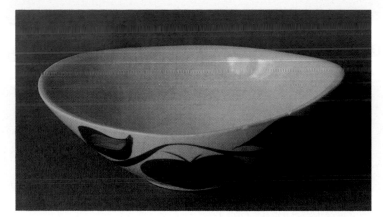

Oval Bowl:
2" high at highest point
5" wide, 6" long
No bottom mark
Rare

Plate 72

#106 Apple Bowl:
3½" high, 10¾" diameter
Marked "WATT 106 USA ORCHARD WARE"

Apple Chip 'n Dip Set:
This chip and dip set has a #120 bowl on the top and a #96 bowl on the bottom. Although many collectors have this combination, it is incorrect. The bottom bowl should be a #110 which is similar in shape to the #120. Price and description will be for the correct #120/#110 set.

Small bowl #120:
2" high, 5" diameter
Marked "WATT ORCHARD WARE 120 USA"

Large bowl #110:
3¾" high, 8" diameter
Marked "WATT ORCHARD WARE 110 USA"

Plate 73

Plate 74

Apple Ribbed Bowls (left to right):

#602 – 1¾" high, 4¾" diameter
Marked "WATT OVEN WARE 602 USA"

#604 – 2½" high, 6¾" diameter
Marked "WATT OVEN WARE 604 USA"

#603 – 2" high, 5¾" diameter
Marked "WATT OVEN WARE 603 USA"

Note: Bowls #600 (7¾" diameter) and #601 (8¾" diameter) complete this nesting set.
See plate 92.

Plate 75

Apple Ribbed Mixing Bowls (left to right):

#9 – (not pictured)
5" high, 9" diameter
Marked "WATT OVEN WARE 9 USA"

#6 – 3½" high, 6" diameter
Marked "WATT OVEN WARE 6 USA"

#8 – 4½" high, 8" diameter
Marked "WATT OVEN WARE 8 USA"

#5 – 2¾" high, 5" diameter
Marked "WATT OVEN WARE 5 USA"

#7 – 4" high, 7" diameter
Marked "WATT OVEN WARE 7 USA"

Plate 76

Apple Mixing Bowls (largest to smallest):

#9 – 5" high, 9" diameter
Marked "WATT OVEN WARE 9 USA"

#8 – 4½" high, 8" diameter
Marked "WATT OVEN WARE 8 USA"

#7 – 4" high, 7" diameter
Marked "WATT OVEN WARE 7 USA"

#6 – 3½" high, 6" diameter
Marked "WATT OVEN WARE 6 USA"

#5 – 2¾" high, 5" diameter
Marked "WATT OVEN WARE 5 USA"

Apple Mixing Bowls (left to right):   Plate 77

#65 – 5¾" high, 8½" diameter
Marked "65 USA"

#64 – 5" high, 7½" diameter
Marked "64 USA"

#63 – 4" high, 6½" diameter
Marked "63 USA"

Apple Ribbed Mixing
Bowls (left to right):
#04 – 2" high, 4"
diameter
Marked "WATT OVEN
WARE 04 USA"

#05 – 2½" high, 5"
diameter
Marked "WATT OVEN
WARE 05 USA"

Plate 78

#06 – 3" high, 6" diameter
Marked "WATT OVEN WARE 06 USA"

#07 – 3¾" high, 7" diameter
Marked "WATT OVEN WARE 07 USA"

#39 Apple Spaghetti Bowl
3" high, 13" diameter
Marked "39 USA" or "OVEN WARE R-F
SPAGHETTI 39"

Plate 79

(left)
#73 Apple Bowl :
4" high, 9½" diameter
Marked "OVEN WARE 73 USA"
Narrow green band around
outside (see note on #73
Casserole, pg. 53)

(right):
#55 Apple Bowl:
4" high, 11¾" diameter
Marked "OVEN WARE 55 USA"

Plate 80

Plate 81

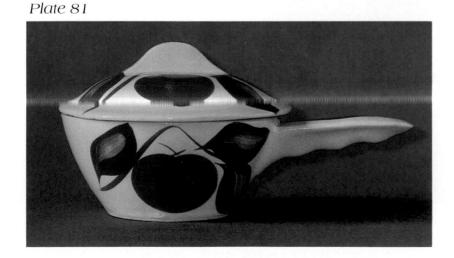

#18 Apple French-Handled Individual
Casserole:
4" high, 8" long
Marked "WATT OVEN WARE 18"

46

Plate 82

A comparison of two apple individual serving casseroles (left to right):

#18 Apple Stick-Handled Casserole:
3¾" high, 7½" long
Marked "18 USA"

#18 Apple French-Handled Individual Casserole
(See description for Plate 81)

Plate 83

Apple Fondue:
3" high, 9" long
Marked "MADE IN USA"
Rare

#18 Tab-Handled Individual Casserole:
4" high, 5" diameter
Marked "18 USA"

Plate 84

47

Plate 85

#05 Apple Covered Bowl, Ribbed:
4" high, 5" diameter
Marked "WATT OVEN WARE 05 USA"

Plate 86

#01 Apple Grease Jar:
5½" high, 5¼" diameter
Marked "WATT OVEN WARE 01 USA"
Rare

Plate 87

#503 Apple Cookie Jar:
8¼" high, 8¼" diameter
Marked "WATT OVEN WARE 503 USA"

Plate 88

#21 Apple Cookie Jar:
7½" high, 7" diameter at top
Marked "OVEN WARE 21 USA"

Plate 89

#76 Apple Two-Handled Bean
Pot:
6½" high, 7½" diameter
Marked "WATT OVEN WARE 76
USA"

#75 Apple Individual Bean Server:
2¼" high, 3½" diameter
Marked "OVEN WARE 75 USA"

Plate 90

Apple Casserole Warmers:
2" high, 7" diameter
No bottom mark
On top is stenciled, "NOTICE – PLEASE DO NOT IMMERSE THIS UNIT IN WATER"
Extremely Rare

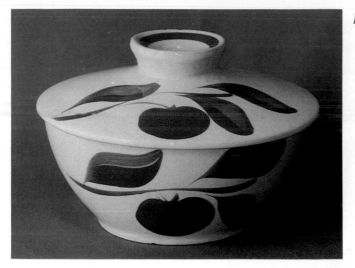

Plate 91

#131 Apple Covered Bowl:
6¼" high, bowl diameter 8½", lid diameter 9"
Marked "WATT 131 USA ORCHARD WARE"

Plate 92

(left)
#600 Apple Ribbed
Covered Bowl:
5½" high, 7¾" diameter
Marked "WATT OVEN
WARE 600 USA"

(right)
#601 Apple Ribbed
Covered Bowl:
6½" high, 8¾" diameter
Marked "WATT OVEN
WARE 601 USA"

Note: These bowls were also used without the covers in a nesting set #600 through #604

Plate 93

#96 Apple Covered Baker, Small Handle:
5¾" high, 8½" diameter
Marked "WATT OVEN WARE 96 USA"

Plate 94

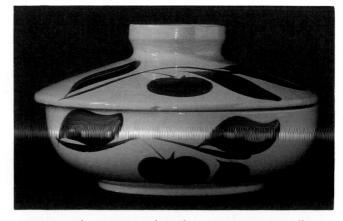

#96 Apple Covered Baker, Large Handle:
5½" high, 8½" diameter
Marked "WATT OVEN WARE 96 USA"

Plate 95

Plate 96

Apple Ice Bucket:
7¼" high, 7½" diameter
No bottom mark

#80 Apple Cheese Crock:
8" high, 8½" diameter
Marked "OVEN WARE 80 USA"

#72 Large Apple Canister:
9½" high, 7" diameter
Marked "OVEN WARE 72 USA"

Plate 97

Plate 98

#91 Apple Dome-Top Canister:
10¾" high, 7½" diameter
Marked "WATT OVEN WARE 91 USA"
Rare

Plate 99

#67 Apple Covered Bowl:
6½" high, 8½" diameter
Marked "OVEN WARE 67 USA"

Plate 100

Apple Canister Set: (left to right)

#81 Flour and Sugar Canisters:
8" high, 6½" diameter
Marked "OVEN WARE 81 USA"

#82 Tea and Coffee Canisters:
7" high, 5" diameter
Marked "OVEN WARE 82 USA"
All extremely rare

Plate 101

#3/19 Apple Casserole On Stand:
Casserole is 5¼" high, 8½" diameter
Stand is 3½" high, 5½" diameter
Marked "OVEN WARE 3/19 USA"

Plate 102

#73 Apple Dutch Oven Casserole:
6" high, bottom diameter 9½", lid
diameter 10¼"
Marked "OVEN WARE 73 USA"

Note: The #73 mold doubled as the bottom of this casserole and as a large salad bowl. It was made with the apple on the outside, on the bottom of the inside and with just the green stripe on the outside. The bowl with the apple on the inside should not be used with the casserole lid.

#62 Double Apple Creamer:
4¼" high, 4½" wide
Marked "62 USA"

Plate 103

Plate 104

#96 Double Apple Covered Baker on Stand:
Covered baker 5½" high, 8½" diameter
Marked "WATT OVEN WARE 96 USA"
Stand is 2¼" high

Plate 105

Reduced Decoration Apple
Mixing Bowls:
(left)
#63 – 4" high, 6½" diameter
Marked "OVEN WARE 63 USA"

(right)
#64 – 5" high, 7½" diameter
Marked "OVEN WARE 64 USA"

Plate 106

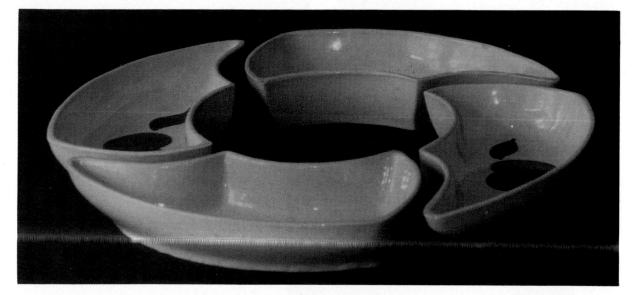

Reduced Decoration Apple Lazy Susan Set:
Each piece is 8½" long at its longest point, 4¼" wide at its widest point, and 1½"
high. If placed together they make a circle 13" in diameter.
No bottom mark
Note: This set probably came on a wooden base and had a circular center piece,
but no information has been found on this to date.
Extremely rare

Plate 107

Double Apple Mixing Bowls:

#04 – 2" high, 4" diameter
Marked "WATT OVEN WARE 04 USA"

#05 – 2½" high, 5" diameter
Marked "WATT OVEN WARE 05 USA"

#06 – 3" high, 6" diameter
Marked "WATT OVEN WARE 06 USA"

#07 – 3¾" high, 7" diameter
Marked "WATT OVEN WARE 07 USA"

Plate 108

#73 Double Apple Bowl:
4" high, 9" diameter
Marked "OVEN WARE 73 USA"

Open Apple Mixing Bowls:
(largest to smallest)

Plate 109

#8 – 4½" high, 8" diameter
Marked "WATT OVEN WARE
8 USA"

#7 – 4" high, 7" diameter
Marked "WATT OVEN WARE
7 USA"

#6 – 3½" high, 6" diameter
Marked "WATT OVEN WARE
6 USA"

#5 – 2¾" high, 5" diameter
Marked "WATT OVEN WARE
5 USA"

Rare

CHAPTER FIVE

Starflower Series

The Starflower series was introduced in the early 1950's and, like the Apple and Pansy series, there were several variations. The best known and most popular is the deep red Starflower with green leaves on the cream-colored pottery, but there are two very different styles of this red flower.

One style has four long, narrow, red petals forming a poinsettia-type flower with a small green center and two large green leaves. The other style, somewhat more complicated, has a red flower with five roundish petals which come to a point at the tips and a small green center. It has three large green leaves, instead of two, and a small red bud on the tip of a narrow stem bending to the left. Both styles appear in the pages that follow and will be referred to as Starflower.

These same starflower patterns appeared on pottery in different color combinations. The patterns are not as colorful as the above-described, as they appear in all one color on various contrasting colors of pottery. Pictured in this chapter are light-green on brown ("Silhouette"), pale pink on green or black ("Moonflower"), and white on red, green or blue. It should be noted that the pale pink on green or black sometimes appears to be white. Thus another example of the individuality and uniqueness of Watt pottery.

Both versions of the "Red Starflower"

Multi-Color Glazed Dinnerware With Starflower Pattern

Plate 110

(back)
#76 Starflower Two-
Handled Bean Pot:
6½" high, 7½" diameter
Marked "OVEN WARE 76
USA"

(front)
#75 Starflower Individual
Bean Servers:
2¼" high, 3½" diameter
Marked "OVEN WARE 75
USA"

Plate 111

#47 Starflower Grease Jar:
5" high, 4½" diameter
Marked "47"

Plate 112

#56 Starflower Tumblers:
(left)
Round-sided Tumbler:
4" high, 3½" diameter
Marked "56"

(right)
Slant-sided Tumbler:
4½" high, 4" diameter
Marked "56 USA"

Plate 113

Starflower Mugs:
(left)
#121 Starflower Mug:
3¾" high, 3" diameter
Marked "WATT 121 USA"

(right)
#501 Starflower Mug:
4½" high, 2¾" diameter
Marked "WATT 501 USA"

Starflower Salt and Pepper
Sets: (left to right)

Barrel-Shaped S/P (red/green
bands)
4" high, 2½" diameter

Hourglass S/P (Raised letters
on front)
4½" high, 2½" diameter

Barrel-Shaped S/P (green
bands)
4" high, 2½" diameter

Plate 114

Plate 116

Plate 115

#18 Starflower Stick-Handled Individual Casserole:
3¾" high, 7½" long
Marked "18 USA"

Starflower Ice Bucket:
7¼" high, 7½" diameter
No bottom mark

#18 Starflower French-Handled Individual Casserole:
4" high, 8" long
Marked "WATT OVEN WARE 18"

Plate 117

Plate 118

#18 Starflower Tab-Handled Individual Casserole:
4" high, 5" diameter
Marked "18 USA"

Plate 119

This photo compares the tiny Starflower creamer to the various pitchers that Watt offered (left to right):

#62 Starflower Creamer:
4¼" high, 4½" wide
Marked "62"

#16 Starflower Pitcher:
6½" high, 6¾" wide
Marked "16 USA"

#15 Starflower Pitcher:
5½" high, 5¾" wide
Marked "OVEN WARE 15 USA"

#17 Starflower Ice-Lip Pitcher:
8" high, 8½" wide
Marked "17 USA"

60

Plate 120

#17 Starflower Ice-Lip Pitcher;
(four petaled variation of #17 pitcher
listed on bottom of page 60)
8" high, 8½" wide
Marked "17 USA"

Plate 121

#69 Starflower Refrigerator
Pitcher (square-shaped):
8" high, 8½" wide
Marked "69 USA"

Plate 122

Starflower Berry Bowls:
1 ½" high, 5¾" diameter
Marked "WATT USA"

61

#74 Starflower Cereal/Salad Bowl:
2" high, 5½" diameter
Marked "OVEN WARE 74 USA"

Plate 123

Plate 124

#64 Starflower Bowl:
3" high, 7½" diameter
Marked "64 USA"

Plate 125

#73 Starflower Bowl:
4" high, 9½" diameter
Marked "OVEN WARE 73 USA"

#39 Starflower Bowl:
3" high, 13" diameter
Marked "OVEN WARE 39 USA"

Plate 126

Plate 127

#33 Starflower Pie Plate:
1½" high, 9" diameter
Marked "EVE-N-BAKE OVEN WARE
33 USA"

Plate 128

#31 Starflower Platter:
15" diameter
Marked "31 USA"

#54 Starflower Covered Casserole:
6" high, 8½" diameter
Marked "OVEN WARE 54 USA"

Plate 129

Plate 130

#21 Starflower Cookie Jar:
7½" high, 7" diameter at top
Marked "OVEN WARE 21 USA"

Plate 131

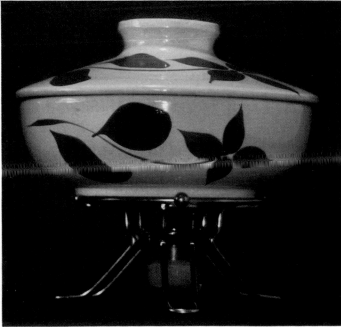

#96 Starflower Covered Baker
On Warming Stand:
5½" high, 8½" diameter
(Stand is 3½" high, 6½" diameter)
Marked "WATT OVEN WARE 96 USA"

Plate 132

Starflower Mixing Bowls (left to right):

#6 – 3" high, 6" diameter
Marked "OVEN WARE 6 USA"

#7 – 3½" high, 7" diameter
Marked "OVEN WARE 7 USA"

#8 – 4" high, 8" diameter
Marked "OVEN WARE 8 USA"

Not pictured: #5 (5" diameter), #9 (9" diamteer)

Plate 133

Starflower Bowls (left to right):

#52 – Cereal/Salad Bowl:
2½" high, 6½" diameter
Marked "OVEN WARE 52 USA"

#53 – 3" high, 7½" diameter
Marked "OVEN WARE 53 USA"

#54 – 3½" high, 8½" diameter
Marked "OVEN WARE 54 USA"

Plate 134

Starflower Mixing Bowls (left to right):

#04 – 2" high, 4" diameter
Marked "WATT OVEN WARE 04 USA"

#06 – 3" high, 6" diameter
Marked "WATT OVEN WARE 06 USA"

#05 – 2½" high, 5" diameter
Marked "WATT OVEN WARE 05 USA"

#07 – (not pictured)
3¾" high, 7" diameter
Marked "WATT OVEN WARE 07 USA"

(left)
#56 Green-On-Brown Starflower Tumbler:
4½" high, 4" diameter at top
Marked "56"

(right)
#17 Green-On-Brown Starflower Pitcher:
8" high, 8½" wide
Marked "R-F 17 USA"

Plate 135

Plate 136

#5 Green-On-Brown Starflower Mixing Bowl:
2¾" high, 5" diameter
Marked "OVEN WARE 5 USA"

Note: This bowl is part of a nesting set #5 through #9.)

Plate 137

(left to right)
#15 Green-On-Brown Starflower Pitcher:
5½" high, 5¾" wide
Marked "OVEN WARE 15 USA"

#18 Green-On-Brown Starflower Tab Handled Individual Casserole:
4" high, 5" diameter
Marked "18 USA"

#16 Green-On-Brown Starflower Pitcher:
6½" high, 6¾" wide
Marked "16 USA"

Plate 138

#39 Green-On-Brown Starflower Spaghetti Bowl:
3" high, 13" diameter
Marked "OVEN WARE 39 USA"

Plate 139

#54 Green-On-Brown Starflower
Covered Casserole:
6" high, 8½" diameter
Marked "OVEN WARE 54 USA"

Plate 140

#21 Green-On-Brown Starflower Cookie Jar:
7½" high, 7" diameter at top
Marked "OVEN WARE 21 USA"

Plate 141

#31 Green-On-Brown Starflower Platter:
15" diameter
Marked "WATT USA"

Plate 142

Pink-On-Green Starflower
Bread Plate:
6½" diameter
Marked "WATT USA"

Pink-On-Green Starflower Dinner Plate:
10" diameter
Marked "WATT USA"

Plate 143

*Pink-On-Green Starflower
Berry Bowls:
1 ¾" high, 5" diameter
Marked "WATT USA"*

Plate 144

Plate 145

*Pink-On-Green Starflower Cup
and Saucer:
Cup - 2¾" high, 4½" diameter
Saucer – 6" diameter
Both pieces marked "WATT "*

Plate 146

*Pink-On-Green Starflower Berry
Set On Spinning Wood Base:
Large Covered Bowl:
4¾" high, 8¾" diameter
Marked "WATT OVEN WARE
USA "*

*Berry Bowls:
1 ¾" high, 5" diameter
Marked "WATT USA "*

Pink-On-Black Starflower Bowl:
2½" high, 11" diameter
Marked "WATT OVEN WARE USA"

Plate 154

Plate 155

Pink-On-Black Starflower Cup and Saucer:
Cup – 2¾ " high, 4½" diameter
Saucer – 6" diameter
Both pieces marked "WATT"

Plate 156

Pink-On-Black Starflower Sugar:
2¾ " high, 6½" wide
Marked "WATT USA"

Plate 157

#39 White-On-Red Starflower Spaghetti Bowl:
3" high, 13" diameter
Marked "OVEN WARE R-F SPAGHETTI 39"
Extremely Rare

#121 White-On-Red Starflower Mug:
3¾" high, 3" diameter
Marked "WATT 121 USA"
Extremely Rare

Plate 159

Plate 158

#39 White-On-Blue Starflower Spaghetti
Bowl:
3" high, 13" diameter
Marked "OVEN WARE R-F SPAGHETTI 39"
Extremely Rare

CHAPTER SIX

Tulip/Dutch Tulip Series

In the mid 1950's, after the introduction of the Starflower and Apple series, the Watts designed and produced still another popular line of which there were two distinct versions — the Tulip and Dutch Tulip. The standard Tulip pattern introduced a bold, colorful flower design — one large royal blue tulip leaning to the left and one large deep red tulip leaning to the right, with slender deep green leaves between and on either side of these flowers. The Dutch Tulip pattern has a rather "folk art" appearance with its cobalt blue tulip and small alternating green and red leaves.

It is believed that production of both Tulip versions was rather low because, not only are the pieces relatively scarce, but the variety of items found is very limited. Tulip pattern is fast becoming a favorite of Watt collectors today, second only to the Apple pattern. Its rarity and distinctive beauty make it both challenging and rewarding to collect.

Examples of the Tulip Series

Examples of the Dutch Tulip Series

Plate 160

#15 Tulip Pitcher:
5½" high, 5¾" wide
Marked "WATT 15 MADE IN USA"
Extremely rare

Plate 161

(front) #62 Tulip Creamer:
4¼" high, 4½" wide
Marked "62 USA"

(back left) #16 Tulip Pitcher:
6½" high, 6¾" wide
Marked "16 USA"

(back right) #17 Tulip Ice-Lip
Pitcher:
8" high, 8½" wide
Marked "17 USA"

Plate 162

Tulip Mixing Bowls: (left to right)
#63 – 4" high, 6½" diameter
Marked "OVEN WARE 63 USA"

#64 – 5" high, 7½" diameter
Marked "OVEN WARE 64 USA"

#65 – 5¾" high, 8½" diameter
Marked "OVEN WARE 65 USA"

Plate 163

#603 Tulip Bowl:
2" high, 5¾" diameter
Marked "WATT OVEN WARE 603 USA"

Note: This bowl is part of a nesting set.
Other bowls are:
#600 (7¾" diameter),
#601 (8¾" diameter),
#602 (4¾" diameter),
#604 (6¾" diameter)

#600 Tulip Ribbed Covered Bowl:
5½" high, 7¾" diameter
Marked "WATT OVEN WARE 600 USA"

Note: This bowl was also used in the nesting set #600 through #604.

Plate 164

Plate 165

#73 Tulip Bowl:
4" high, 9½" diameter
Marked "OVEN WARE 73 USA"

Plate 166

#503 Tulip Cookie Jar:
8¼" high, 8¼" diameter
Marked "WATT OVEN WARE 503 USA"

Dutch Tulip Divided Plate:
10½" diameter
No bottom mark
Extremely rare

Plate 167

(left to right)
#62 Dutch Tulip Creamer:
4¼" high, 4½" wide
Marked "62"

#15 Dutch Tulip Pitcher:
5½" high, 5¾" wide
Marked "OVEN WARE 15 USA"

#16 Dutch Tulip Pitcher:
6½" high, 6¾" wide
Marked "16 USA"

Plate 168

#69 Dutch Tulip Refrigerator Pitcher (square-shaped):
8" high, 8½" wide
Marked "69 USA"

Plate 169

Plate 170

#18 Dutch Tulip French-Handled Individual Casserole:
4" high, 8" long
Marked "WATT OVEN WARE 18"

Plate 171

#05 Dutch Tulip Covered Bowl:
4" high, 5" diameter
Marked "WATT OVEN WARE 05"

Plate 172

Dutch Tulip Mixing Bowls:
#63 – 4" high, 6½" diameter
Marked "OVEN WARE 63 USA"

#64 – 5" high, 7½" diameter
Marked "OVEN WARE 64 USA"

#65 – 5¾" high, 8½" diameter
Marked "OVEN WARE 65 USA"

Plate 173

#6 Dutch Tulip Bowl:
3½" high, 6" diameter
Marked "OVEN WARE 6 USA"

Note: This bowl is part of a nesting set #5 through #9.

Plate 174

Dutch Tulip Serving Set:
(center)
#66 Dutch Tulip Covered Bowl.
5½" high, 7½" diameter
Marked "OVEN WARE 66 USA"

(outside)
#68 Dutch Tulip Bowls:
1¾" high, 5" diameter
Marked "OVEN WARE 68 USA"

#67 Dutch Tulip Covered Bowl:
6½" high, 8½" diameter
Marked "67 USA"

Plate 176

Plate 175

#76 Dutch Tulip Two-Handled Bean Pot:
6½" high, 7½" diameter
Marked "OVEN WARE 76 USA"

Plate 177

#80 Dutch Tulip Cheese Crock:
8" high, 8½" diameter
Marked "OVEN WARE 80 USA"

Plate 178

#39 Dutch Tulip Spaghetti Bowl:
3" high, 13" diameter
Marked "OVEN WARE 39 R-F
SPAGHETTI"

Plate 179

Dutch Tulip Canister Set:
(left to right)
#81 Flour and Sugar
Canisters:
8" high, 6½" diameter
Marked "OVEN WARE 81
USA"

#82 Tea and Coffee
Canisters:
7" high, 5" diameter
Marked "OVEN WARE 82
USA"
All extremely rare

CHAPTER SEVEN

Cherry Series

The Cherry series was introduced in the mid 1950's. Production was probably very low because these pieces are not easily found and variety of molds is limited. The Cherry pattern is very colorful and has the same homespun look as many of the previous lines. Deep red cherries hang from a thin swooping green stem on the right side, while a deep red six-petaled flower with a yellow center appears at the left side, with two large green leaves in between.

#15 Cherry Pitcher :
"Salesman's Sample"

Plate 180

Plate 181

(left)
#15 Cherry Pitcher w/advertising:
5½" high, 5¾" wide
Marked "OVEN WARE !5 USA"

(right)
#17 Cherry Pitcher:
8" high, 8½" wide
Marked "RF 17 USA"

#21 Cherry Cookie Jar:
7½" high, 7" diameter at top
Marked "OVEN WARE 21 USA"

Plate 182

Plate 183

#3/19 Cherry Covered Casserole:
5" high, 9" diameter
Marked "OVEN WARE 3/19 USA"

Plate 184

#39 Cherry Spaghetti Bowl:
3" high, 13" diameter
Marked "OVEN WARE 39 USA"

#31 Cherry Platter:
15" diameter
Marked "WATT USA"

Plate 185

Plate 186

#23 Cherry Cereal/Salad Bowl:
(Cherry on inside of bowl)
1½" high, 5¾" diameter
Marked "WATT 23 USA"

Plate 187

Cherry Mixing Bowls:
(left)
#6 – 3" high, 6" diameter
Marked "OVEN WARE 6 USA"

(right)
#8 – 4" high, 8" diameter
Marked "OVEN WARE 8 USA"

Note: These bowls are part of
a nesting set #5 through #9.

#4 Cherry Berry Bowl:
2" high, 5" diameter
Marked "OVEN WARE 4 USA"

Plate 188

Plate 189

#52 Cherry Cereal/Salad Bowls:
2½" high, 6½" diameter
Marked "OVEN WARE 52 USA"

Plate 190

Cherry Barrel-Shaped Salt Shaker:
4" high, 2½" diameter
No bottom mark
(This shaker was sold as part of a
popcorn set, thus a pepper shaker
was not made in this pattern)

84

CHAPTER EIGHT

Tear Drop/American Red Bud Series

The Tear Drop or American Red Bud series was introduced in the mid 1950's. Many collectors have called it the Bleeding Heart pattern. This is a very simple, yet striking pattern with deep red drooping buds resembling rosebuds, light brown stems, and small deep green leaves. Pieces in this pattern seem fairly difficult to locate, however, there seems to be a wide variety of pieces, sometimes in molds that are extremely rare in most other patterns. Somewhat of a sleeper now, we believe this pattern will gain considerable popularity as more collectors discover its wonderful color and beauty.

Plate 191

Tear Drop Serving Set:

(center)
#73 Tear Drop Bowl:
4" high, 9½" diameter
Marked "OVEN WARE 73 USA"

(outside)
#74 Tear Drop Bowls:
2" high, 5½" diameter
Marked "OVEN WARE 74 USA"

(left to right)
#62 Tear Drop Creamer:
4¼" high, 4½" wide
Marked "62"

#15 Tear Drop Pitcher:
5½" high, 5¾" wide
Marked "OVEN WARE 15 USA"

#16 Tear Drop Pitcher
6½" high, 6¾" wide
Marked "16 USA"

Plate 192

#69 Tear Drop Refrigerator Pitcher
(square-shaped)
8" high, 8½" wide
Marked "69 USA"

Plate 193

Plate 194

Tear Drop Barrel-Shaped Salt and Pepper
4" high, 2½" diameter
No bottom mark

#18 Tear Drop French-Handled Individual Casserole:
4" high, 8" long
Marked "WATT OVEN WARE 18"

Plate 195

Plate 196

#76 Tear Drop Two-Handled Bean Pot:
6½" high, 7½" diameter
Marked "WATT OVEN WARE 76 USA"

#75 Tear Drop Individual Bean Server:
2¼" high, 3½" diameter
Marked "WATT OVEN WARE 75 USA"

Tear Drop Square-Shaped Covered Casserole:
6" high, 8" wide
No bottom mark
Rare

Plate 197

#80 Tear Drop Cheese Crock:
8" high, 8¼" diameter
Marked "OVEN WARE 80 USA"

Plate 198

Plate 199

#86 Tear Drop Covered
Casserole (Oval-shaped):
5" high, 10" diameter
Marked "WATT OVEN WARE
86 USA"
Extremely rare

Plate 200

#66 Tear Drop Bowl:
3" high, 7" diameter
Marked "OVEN WARE 66 USA"

Plate 201

Note: These bowls are part of a nesting set. Other bowls are: #5 (5" diameter), #8 (8" diameter), #9 (9" diameter).

Tear Drop Mixing Bowls:

(left to right)
#6 – 3½" high, 6" diameter
Marked "WATT OVEN WARE 6 USA"

#7 – 4" high, 7" diameter
Marked "WATT OVEN WARE 7 USA"

Plate 202

Tear Drop Mixing Bowls:
(left to right)
#05 – 2½" high, 5" diameter
Marked "WATT OVEN WARE 05 USA"

#07 – 3¾" high, 7" diameter
Marked "WATT OVEN WARE 07 USA"

Note: These bowls are part of a nesting set. Not pictured are: #04 (4" diameter) and #06 (6" diameter).

Plate 203

Tear Drop Mixing Bowls:
#63 – 4¼" high, 6½" diameter
Marked "OVEN WARE 63 USA"

#64 – 5" high, 7½" diameter
Marked "OVEN WARE 64 USA"

Note: These bowls are part of a nesting set. Not pictured is: #65 (5¾" high, 8½" diameter).

CHAPTER NINE

Rooster Series

The Rooster pattern, introduced in 1955, is probably the best example of the individuality and uniqueness of Watt pottery. A favorite in the Midwest farm belt, a rooster outlined in black with green and red feathers standing in the grass is hand-painted on these popular pieces. This pattern is somewhat scarce, but there seems to be a good variety of pieces available.

#69 Rooster Refrigerator Pitcher:
(Square-Shaped)
8" high, 8½" wide
Marked "69 USA"

Plate 204

Plate 205

(left)
#15 Rooster Pitcher:
5½" high, 5¾" wide
Marked "OVEN WARE 15 USA"

(right)
#16 Rooster Pitcher:
6½" high, 6¾" wide
Marked "16 USA"

Plate 206

#05 Rooster Covered Bowl:
4" high, 5" diameter
Marked "WATT OVEN WARE 05 USA"

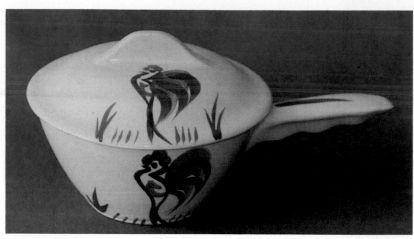

Plate 207

#18 Rooster French-Handled
Individual Casserole:
4" high, 8" long
Marked "WATT OVEN WARE 18"

Plate 208

(left)
Rooster Hourglass
Salt/Pepper:
(holes on top depict "S"
and "P")
4½" high, 2½" diameter

(right)
Rooster Barrel-Shaped
Salt/Pepper
4" high, 2½" diameter

No bottom marks on
either

Plate 209

#98 Rooster Covered
Sugar:
4½" high, 5" wide, 3¼"
diameter at opening
Marked "98 USA"

#62 Rooster Creamer:
4¼" high, 4½" wide,
Marked "62"

Plate 210

Rooster Canister Set: (left to right)

#81 Flour and Sugar Canisters:
8" high, 6½" diameter
Marked "OVEN WARE 81 USA"
(Flour canister not pictured)

#82 Tea and Coffee Canisters:
7" high, 5" diameter
Marked "OVEN WARE 82 USA"
All extremely rare

Plate 212

Plate 211

#76 Rooster Two-Handled Bean Pot:
6½" high, 7½" diameter
Marked "OVEN WARE 76 USA"

Rooster Ice Bucket:
7¼" high, 7½" diameter
No bottom mark

Plate 213

#67 Rooster Covered Bowl:
6½" high, 8½" diameter
Marked "67 USA"

Plate 214

Rooster Nesting Bowls: (left to right)

#68 – 1¾" high, 5" diameter
Marked "68 USA"

#67 – 2½" high, 6" diameter
Marked "67 USA"

#66 – 3" high, 7" diameter
Marked "66 USA"

Plate 215

Rooster Mixing Bowls: (each belongs to a set of nesting bowls)

(left)
#5 – 2¾" high, 5" diameter
Marked "OVEN WARE 5 USA"
(Nesting set includes #5 through #9)

#63 – 4¼" high, 6½" diameter
Marked "63 USA"
(Nesting set includes #63 through #65)

Plate 216

Plate 217

#73 Rooster Bowl:
4" high, 9½" diameter
Marked "OVEN WARE 73 USA"

Plate 218

#58 Rooster Bowl:
3¾" high, 10½" diameter
Marked "OVEN WARE 58 USA"

Plate 220

#67 Rooster Bowl:
3½" high, 8¼" diameter
Marked "67 USA"
(This bowl should have a lid)

Plate 219

Rooster Rectangular Baking Dish:
10" long (handle to handle)
5¼" wide, 2¼" high
No bottom mark
Extremely rare

Rooster Spaghetti Bowl:
3" high, 13" diameter
No bottom mark

95

CHAPTER TEN

Autumn Foliage Series

The Autumn Foliage pattern was introduced in 1959 and has small brown leaves on brown stems. Its simplicity of design and color facilitated a swift and efficient production. These pieces are fairly easy to locate and there is a good variety of pieces to collect. Although not as colorful as some Watt patterns, a collection of Autumn Foliage is very pleasing to the eye and blends attractively with earthtone color schemes.

Plate 221

#100 Autumn Foliage Covered
Sugar:
4½" high, 5" wide, 3" diameter
at top
Marked "98 USA"

#62 Autumn Foliage Creamer:
4¼" high, 4½" wide
Marked "62 USA"

Plate 222

#126 Autumn Foliage Oil/Vinegar Set:
7" high
Marked "126 USA"
(vinegar lid is missing in this photo)

Plate 223

(left)
Autumn Foliage
Hourglass Salt & Pepper:
(holes on top depict "S"
and "P")
4½" high, 2½" diameter

(right)
Autumn Foliage
Hourglass Salt & Pepper:
(raised letters on front)
4¼" high, 2½" diameter

No bottom marks on
these.

(left)
#121 Autumn Foliage Mug:
3¾" high, 3" diameter
Marked "WATT 121 USA"

(right)
#501 Autumn Foliage Mug
4½" high, 2¾" diameter
Marked "WATT 501 USA"

Plate 224

Plate 225

Autumn Foliage Fondue:
3" high, 9" long
Marked "MADE IN USA"

Plate 226

Autumn Foliage Ice Bucket:
7¾" high, 7½" diameter
No bottom mark

#33 Autumn Foliage Pie Plate:
1½" high, 9" diameter
Marked "EVE-N-BAKE OVEN
WARE 33 USA"

Plate 227

Plate 228

#31 Autumn Foliage Platter:
15" diameter
Marked "31 USA"

Plate 229

#96 Autumn Foliage Covered Baker:
5¾" high, 8½" diameter
Marked "WATT OVEN WARE 96 USA"

99

Plate 230

(left to right)
#15 Autumn Foliage Pitcher:
5½" high, 5¾" wide
Marked "OVEN WARE 15 USA"

#16 Autumn Foliage Pitcher:
6½" high, 6¾" wide
Marked "16 USA"

#17 Autumn Foliage Ice-Lip
Pitcher:
8" high, 8½" wide
Marked "WATT 17 USA"

#5 Autumn Foliage Ribbed Bowl:
2¾" high, 5" diameter
Marked "WATT OVEN WARE 5 USA"
Note: This bowl is part of a nesting
set. Other bowls are:
#6 (6" diameter),
#7 (7" diameter),
#8 (8" diameter),
#9 (9" diameter)

Plate 231

Plate 232

#600 Autumn Foliage Ribbed Bowl:
3" high, 7¾" diameter
Marked "WATT OVEN WARE 600 USA"
Note: This bowl is part of a nesting set.
Other bowls are:
#601 (8¾" diameter,)
#602 (4¾" diameter),
#603 (5¾" diameter),
#604 (6¾" diameter)

Plate 233

Autumn Foliage Mixing Bowls:
(left to right)

#65 – 5¾" high, 8½" diameter
Marked "OVEN WARE 65 USA"

#63 – 4¼" high, 6½" diameter
Marked "OVEN WARE 63 USA"

Note: These bowls are part of a
nesting set. Not pictured is:
#64 (7½" diameter)

#94 Autumn Foliage Cereal
Bowl:
1¾" high, 6" diameter
Marked "WATT OVEN
WARE 94 USA"

Plate 234

Plate 235

#73 Autumn Foliage Bowl:
4" high, 9½" diameter
Marked "OVEN WARE 73 USA"

Plate 236

#106 Autumn Foliage Bowl:
3½" high, 10¾" diameter
Marked "WATT ORCHARD WARE 106 USA"

Plate 237

#505 Autumn Foliage Teapot:
5¾" high, 9" diameter
Marked "WATT OVEN WARE MADE
IN USA"
Extremely rare

Plate 238

#76 Autumn Foliage Two-Handled
Bean Pot:
6½" high, 7½" diameter
Marked "WATT OVEN WARE 76 USA"

Plate 239

#02 Autumn Foliage Refrigerator
Dish:
3" high, 7½" diameter
Marked "WATT OVEN WARE 02 USA"
Note: This piece is part of a 3-piece
refrigerator set.
Rare

CHAPTER ELEVEN

Morning Glory Series

The Morning Glory pattern was produced in the late 1950's and pieces are extremely scarce today. The pottery has an embossed lattice design with raised Morning Glory flowers and leaves. Several color combinations which are illustrated in this chapter include a red flower and green leaves on either cream or yellow glazed pottery, or a cream-colored lattice and flower design on a light brown background. It should be noted that the numbering system used on some Morning Glory pieces differed from that of other Watt lines. Production and variety were very limited in this pattern and these pieces demand premium prices.

Plate 240

#94 Yellow Morning Glory
Casserole: (lid missing)
3¾" high, 8½" diameter
Marked "WATT OVEN WARE
94 USA"

Plate 241

Yellow Morning Glory Mixing
Bowls: (left to right)
#6 – 3½" high, 6" diameter
Marked "WATT OVEN WARE 6
USA"

#7 – 4" high, 7" diameter
Marked "WATT OVEN WARE 7
USA"

Note: These bowls are part of a nesting set. Other bowls
are: #5 (5" diameter), #8 (8" diameter), #9 (9" diameter)

Plate 242

#96 Morning Glory Ice-Lip Pitcher:
8" high, 8½" wide
Marked "WATT OVEN WARE 96 USA"
Note: #96 in other Watt patterns is a
square-shaped refrigerator pitcher. We
believe that this was the only pitcher
offered in this pattern.

Plate 243

(left to right)
#98 Morning Glory
Sugar:
4¼" high, 5" wide, 3"
diameter at opening
Marked "98"

#97 Morning Glory
Creamer:
4¼" high, 4½" wide
Marked "97"

Note: There is a strong possibility that a lid was never offered for this sugar. Also, please note that this creamer is not a #62 like other Watt creamers.

Morning Glory Mixing
Bowls: (largest to smallest)
#9 – 5" high, 9" diameter
Marked "WATT OVEN
WARE 9 USA"

#8 – 4½" high, 8" diameter
Marked "WATT OVEN
WARE 8 USA"

#7 – 4" high, 7" diameter
Marked "WATT OVEN
WARE 7 USA"

#6 – 3½" high, 6" diameter
Marked "WATT OVEN WARE 6 USA"

Not pictured #5 (5" diameter)

Plate 244

Pl

#95 Morning Glory Cookie Jar:
10¾" high, 7½" diameter
Marked "WATT OVEN WARE 95 USA"

Plate 245

N

Plate 250

Eagle Cereal Bowl:
2" high, 5½" diameter
Marked "OVEN WARE 74 USA"

Plate 251

#73 Eagle Bowl:
4" high, 9½" diameter
Marked "OVEN WARE 73 USA"

Plate 252

Plate 253

Dogwood Bread Plate:
6½" diameter
Marked "WATT USA"

#31 Dogwood Platter:
15" diameter
Marked "WATT USA"

Plate 254

Plate 255

White Daisy Salad Plate:
8½" diameter
Marked "WATT USA"

Dogwood Serving Bowl:
3" high, 15" diameter
Marked "WATT OVEN WARE USA"

Plate 257

Plate 256

White Daisy Cup and Saucer:
Cup – 2¾" high, 4½" diameter
Saucer – 6" diameter
Both marked "WATT"

White Daisy Pitcher:
7" high, 7¾" wide
Marked "EVE-N-BAKE WATT WARE OVEN WARE USA"

Plate 258

White Daisy Stick-Handled Individual Casserole:
3¾" high, 7½" long
Marked "WATT OVEN WARE 18"

Plate 259

White Daisy Covered Casserole:
5" high, 8¾" diameter
Marked "WATT OVEN WARE USA"

Plate 260

White Daisy Mixing Bowls: (smallest to largest)

#5 – 2¾" high, 5" diameter
Marked "WATT OVEN WARE 5 USA"

#7 – 4" high, 7" diameter
Marked "WATT OVEN WARE 7 USA"

#8 – 4½" high, 8" diameter
Marked "WATT OVEN WARE 8 USA"

#9 – 5" high, 9" diameter
Marked "WATT OVEN WARE 9 USA"

Not pictured: #6 – (6" diameter)

Plate 261

#7 Butterfly Bowl:
4" high, 7" diameter
Marked "WATT OVEN WARE 7 USA"
Note: This bowl was part of a nesting set.
Apparently very few were made because
they are extremely rare.

Plate 262

Butterfly Ice Bucket (lid missing):
7¼" high, 7½" diameter (with lid)
No bottom mark
Extremely rare

Plate 263

#98 Brown-Banded Covered
Sugar:
4½" high, 5" wide, 3" diameter at
opening
Marked "98"

#62 Brown-Banded Creamer:
4¼" high, 4½" wide
Marked "62 USA"

Plate 264

#121 Brown-Banded Mug:
3¾" high, 3" diameter
Marked "WATT 121 USA"

#112 Brown-Banded Teapot: Plate 265
6" high, 9" wide
Marked "WATT ORCHARD WARE 112 USA"
Extremely rare

#115 Brown-Banded Coffee Pot:
9¾" high, 7" wide
Marked "WATT ORCHARD WARE 115 USA"
Extremely rare

Plate 266

Plate 267

(left)
#102 Brown-Banded Salad Plate:
7½" diameter
Marked "WATT 102 USA"

(right)
#31 Brown-Banded Platter:
15" diameter
Marked "31 USA"

Plate 268

Woodgrain Pitchers:
(left to right)
#613W – 5¾" high, 4½" wide
Marked "OVEN WARE 613W USA"

#614W – 7½" high, 6" wide
Marked "OVEN WARE 614W USA"

#615W – 9" high, 7½" wide
Marked "OVEN WARE 615W USA"

Plate 269

#611W Woodgrain Chip 'n Dip Bowl:
2¾" high, 11¼" diameter
Marked "OVEN WARE 611W USA"
Note: Small bowl is permanently attached to large bowl.

113

Plate 270

Plate 271

#608W Woodgrain Covered Bowl:
7½" high, 9" diameter
Marked "OVEN WARE 608W USA"

#617W Woodgrain Cookie Barrel:
11" high, 8" diameter
Marked "OVEN WARE 617W USA"

Plate 272

Kathy Kale Oval Serving Bowl:
2¾" high, 7¾" wide, 11½" long
Marked "KATHY KALE USA" w/ logo
Rare

Plate 273

Kathy Kale Bowls:
2" high, 5½" diameter
Marked "KATHY KALE
USA" w/ logo
Rare

Kathy Kale Serving Set:
Small bowls – 2" high,
5¼" diameter
Marked "KATHY KALE
USA" w/ logo
Large bowl – 3½" high,
10½" diameter
Marked "USA"
Rare

Plate 274

Plate 275

Green/Brown Leaves Canister Set w/ Wood Lids:
Flour and Sugar – 6" high, 6½" diameter
Coffee and Tea – 5" high, 5" diameter
No bottom marks
Extremely rare
Note: These are the same molds used for the canisters with pottery
lids in Apple, Rooster, and Dutch Tulip patterns.

Plate 276

Snack Bowl Set:

"Nuts" – 1¾" high, 5" diameter   *"Corn" – 2½" high, 6½" diameter*
Marked "OVEN WARE 4 USA"   *Marked "OVEN WARE 52 USA"*

"Chips" – 2¾" high, 7" diameter   *"Pretzels" – 3½" high, 8½" diameter*
Marked "OVEN WARE 7 USA"   *Marked "OVEN WARE 54 USA"*

All Rare

#76 Goodies Jar:
6½" high, 7½" diameter
Marked "WATT OVEN WARE 76 USA"
Rare

Plate 277

Plate 278

#59 Goodies Jar:
8½" high, 7½" diameter
Marked "WATT OVEN WARE 59 USA"
Rare

Plate 279

#72 Goodies Jar:
9½" high, 7½" diameter
Marked "OVEN WARE 72 USA"
Rare

Plate 280

Kla Ham'rd Stacking Refrigerator Jar:
4½" high, 6½" diameter
Marked "OVEN WARE KLA HAM'RD
MADE IN USA"

Plate 281

Kla Ham'rd Bowl:
4½" high, 6½" diameter
Marked "OVEN WARE KLA HAM'RD
M MADE IN USA"

Plate 282

#43-13 Kla Ham'rd Pie Plate:
1½" high, 9" diameter
Marked "OVEN WARE KLA HAM'RD
43-13 MADE IN USA"

(left)
#43-14 Kla Ham'rd Pitcher:
7" high, 8" wide
Marked "OVEN WARE KLA HAM'RD
43-14 MADE IN USA"

(right)
#43-1 Stick-Handled Individual
Casserole:
3½" high, 7" long
Marked "OVEN WARE KLA HAM'RD
43-1 MADE IN USA"

Plate 283

Plate 284

(left)
#43-12 Kla Ham'rd Covered
Casserole:
6½" high, 8" diameter
Marked "OVEN WARE KLA
HAM'RD 43-12 MADE IN USA"

(right)
#43-19 Kla Ham'rd Covered
Casserole:
7½" high, 9" diameter
Marked "OVEN WARE KLA
HAM'RD 43-19 MADE IN USA"

Plate 285

#43-18 Kla Ham'rd Two-Handled
Casserole:
6" high, 9" diameter
Marked "OVEN WARE KLA
HAM'RD 43-18 MADE IN USA"

Plate 286

Multi-Colored Basketweave Mixing Bowls: (smallest to largest)

#5 – 3" high, 5" diameter
Marked "WATT OVEN WARE 5 USA"

#6 – 3½" high, 6" diameter
Marked "WATT OVEN WARE 6 USA"

#7 – 4" high, 7" diameter
Marked "WATT OVEN WARE 7 USA"

#8 – 4½" high, 8" diameter
Marked "WATT OVEN WARE 8 USA"

#9 – 5" high, 9" diameter
Marked "WATT OVEN WARE 9 USA"

Plate 287

Lt. Green Basketweave Serving Set:

(center)
#102 bowl – 4" high, 9½" diameter
Marked "WATT OVEN WARE 102 USA"

(outside)
#100 bowls – 2" high, 5½" diameter
Marked "WATT OVEN WARE 100 USA"

Plate 288   Brown Basketweave Covered Casseroles:

(left)
6¼" high, 8¼" diameter
Marked "JC STONEWARE OVEN
PROOF 805 MADE IN USA"

(right)
6½" high, 8½" diameter
Marked "WATT OVEN WARE 128 USA"
Note: The casserole on the left was made by
Watt for the JC Stoneware Company.

Brown Basketweave Two-Handled Beanpot:
6½" high, 7½" diameter
Marked "JC STONEWARE OVEN PROOF 802 USA"
Note: Made by Watt for the JC Stoneware
Company. It is the same shaped mold as the #76
beanpot.

Plate 290

Plate 289

Brown Basketweave: (left to right)
#806 Mug – 5¼" high, 3¼" diameter
Marked "HEIRLOOM 806 USA"

#801 Mug – 3¾" high, 3¼" diameter
Marked "801 USA"

#100 Bowl – 2" high, 5½" diameter
Marked "WATT OVEN WARE 100
USA"

#814 Ind. Server – 2" high, 7" long
Marked "HEIRLOOM 814 USA"

#810 Ice-Lip Pitcher –
Marked "HEIRLOOM STONEWARE
810"

Note: The pieces marked "Heirloom" were made by Watt for the Heirloom Stoneware Co.

120

Plate 291

#806 Heirloom Brown Basketweave Mug w/ Original Box:
5¼" high, 3¼" diameter
Marked "HEIRLOOM 806 USA"

Plate 292

#806 Heirloom Cream-Colored Basketweave Mug:
5¼" high, 3¼" diameter
Marked "HEIRLOOM 806 USA"
(Made by Watt for the Heirloom Stoneware Co.)

Plate 293

Multi-Colored Swirl-Sided Bowls: (smallest to largest)

#7 4" high, 7" diameter
Marked "WATT OVEN WARE 7 USA"

#8 – 4½" high, 8" diameter
Marked "WATT OVEN WARE 8 USA"

#9 – 5" high, 9" diameter
Marked "WATT OVEN WARE 9 USA"
Not pictured:
#5 (5" diameter),
#6 (6" diameter)

121

Plate 294

(left to right)
#17 Green Swirl-Sided Pitcher:
8" high, 8½" wide
Marked "17 USA"

#21 Green Swirl-Sided Cookie Jar:
7½" high, 7" diameter at top
Marked "OVEN WARE 21 USA"

#9 Green Swirl-Sided Bowl:
5" high, 9" diameter
Marked "OVEN WARE 9 USA"

Plate 295

Multi-Color Panel-Sided Mixing Bowls:
(smallest to largest)
#7 – 2¾" high, 7" diameter
Marked "WATT OVEN WARE 7 USA"

#8 – 4½" high, 8" diameter
Marked "WATT OVEN WARE 8 USA"

#10 – 5" high, 10" diameter
Marked "WATT OVEN WARE 10 USA"

Note: The #7 bowl (front) in this photo
belongs to a different nesting set than
the other two bowls pictured.

Plate 296

White Spray/Teal Green
Casseroles:
(left)
#54 Covered Casserole:
6" high, 8½" diameter
Marked "OVEN WARE 54 USA"

(right)
#18 Tab-Handled Individual
Casserole:
4" high, 5" diameter
Marked "18 USA"

Plate 297

Speckled Watt Ware:
#106 Salad Bowl:
3½" high, 10¾" diameter
Marked "WATT ORCHARD WARE
106 USA"

#120 Bowl: (part of chip 'n dip set)
2" high, 5" diameter
Marked "WATT ORCHARD WARE
120 USA"

Vinegar/Oil Set:
7" high
Marked "126 USA"

Hourglass S/P:
4½" high, 2½" diameter
No bottom marks

Brown Drip Glaze Bowls:
(left)
2¾" high, 8½" diameter
Marked "WATT OVEN WARE
96 USA"

(right)
3½" high, 9" diameter
Marked "WATT OVEN WARE
119 USA"

Plate 298

Plate 299

#96 Brown/Cream Covered Bowl:
5¾" high, 8½" diameter
Marked "WATT OVEN WARE 96
USA"

Plate 300

Plate 301

Cabinart Brown/Cream Covered Pitcher:
6" high, 7" wide
Marked "CABINART BAKE WARE USA" w/ logo
(See chapter 14 for photo of mark)
Note: The Cabinart line was made by Watt and
sold by George Borgfeldt, Inc.

Lt. Green/ Brown Creamer:
4¼" high, 4½" wide
No bottom mark

Plate 303

Plate 302

#62 Olive Green/Brown Creamer:
4¼" high, 4½" wide
Marked "62 USA"

Lt. Green/Brown Pitcher
6½" high, 6¾" wide
No bottom mark

Plate 304

Brown/Green and Brown/Blue Mixing
Bowls:
(smallest to largest)
#5 – 2¾" high, 5" diameter
Marked "WATT OVEN WARE 5 USA"

#6 – 3½" high, 6" diameter
Marked "WATT OVEN WARE 6 USA"

#7 – 4" high, 7" diameter
Marked "WATT OVEN WARE 7 USA"

#8 – 4½" high, 8" diameter
Marked "WATT OVEN WARE 8 USA"

#9 – 5" high, 9" diameter
Marked "WATT OVEN WARE 9 USA"

Plate 305

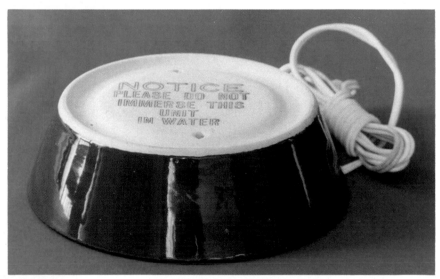

Brown Glaze Electric Warmer:
2" high, 7" diameter
No bottom mark
On top is stenciled, "NOTICE –
PLEASE DO NOT IMMERSE THIS
UNIT IN WATER"

Plate 306

#132 Brown Glaze Carafe:
11" high, 8½" wide
Marked "WATT ORCHARD WARE
132 USA"

125

Plate 307

#602 Brown Glaze Beanpot:
7½" high, 9¼" wide
Marked "WATT OVEN WARE 602 USA"

Plate 308

#7 Brown Glaze Dog Dish:
3" high, 7" diameter
Marked "WATT 7 USA"

Plate 310

Shaded Brown Casserole:
4½" high, 6¾" diameter
Marked "EVE-N-BAKE WATT OVEN WARE USA"

Plate 309

Shaded Brown Mug:
3" high, 3¾" diameter
No bottom mark

Shaded Brown Cookie Jar:
7½" high, 7" diameter at top
Marked "EVE-N-BAKE WATT OVEN WARE USA"

Plate 311

Plate 312

Shaded Brown Pitcher:
7" high, 7¾" wide
Marked "EVE-N-BAKE WATT OVEN
WARE USA"

Plate 313

Shaded Brown Mixing Bowls:
Marked "EVE-N-BAKE WATT OVEN WARE USA"
(left) 4½" high, 6" diameter
(center) 5½" high, 8" diameter
(right) 6½" high, 10" diameter

Plate 314

Shaded Brown Mixing Bowls:
Marked "EVE-N-BAKE WATT OVEN WARE USA"
(left) 2½" high, 5" diameter
(center) 2¾" high, 6" diameter
(right) 3" high, 8" diameter

127

Plate 315

#603 Shaded Brown Mexican Bowl:
2" high, 5½" diameter
Marked "WATT OVEN WARE 603 USA"

Plate 316

Iced Tea Dispenser:
12" high, 8¾" diameter
Marked "MADE IN USA"

Plate 317

Matte-Finish Tea Set:
Teapot – (lid missing)
6" high, 9" wide
Marked "WATT ORCHARD
WARE 112 USA"

Sugar – 4½" high, 5" wide, 3"
diameter at top
Marked "98

Creamer – 4¼" high, 4½" wide
Marked "62"

(back)
#76 Matte-Finish Two-Handled
Bean Pot:
6½" high, 7½" diameter
Marked "WATT OVEN WARE 76
USA"

(front)
#75 Matte-Finish Individual Bean
Servers:
2¼" high, 3½" diameter
Marked "OVEN WARE 75 USA"

Plate 318

#126 Matte-Finish Oil/Vinegar Set w/ Lids:
7" high
Marked "126 USA"

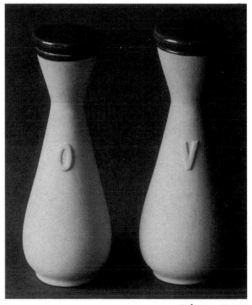

Plate 320

Plate 319

Matte-Finish Salt and Pepper:
4½" high, 2½" diameter
No bottom marks

Plate 321

Matte-Finish Serving Set:

(center)
#73 Bowl – 4" high, 9½" diameter
Marked "WATT OVEN WARE 73 USA"

(outside)
#94 Bowls – 1¾" high, 6" diameter
Marked "WATT OVEN WARE 94 USA"

Esmond Cookie Jar w/ Wood Lid:
8½" high, 7½" diameter
Marked "ESMOND USA"

Plate 322

Plate 323

#36 Esmond Cookie Jar:
8" high, 10" wide
Marked "ESMOND 36 USA"

Plate 324

ESMOND TWO-HANDLED BEAN POT
6½" high, 7½" diameter
Marked "OVEN WARE USA"

Esmond Individual Bean Servers:
Apple, Grape, Pear (Pineapple missing)
2¼" high, 3½" diameter
Marked "OVEN WARE USA"

Plate 325

Esmond Platter:
15" diameter
Marked "USA"

Plate 326

Esmond 4-Section Canister Set On Wood Base w/
Wood Lid:
Set is 10½" high, 10½" diameter
Each section marked "ESMOND 32 USA"

Note: Coffee section has grapes on it.
Tea section has a pear on it.

Plate 327

Plate 328

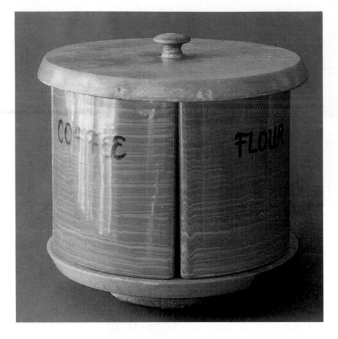

#31 Esmond Grape Mug:
3½" high, 3½" diameter
Marked "ESMOND 31 USA"

Esmond 4-Section Canister Set On Wood
Base w/ Wood Lid:
Each section labeled: "Flour," "Sugar,"
"Coffee", "Tea."
Set is 10½" high, 10½" diameter
Each section marked "ESMOND USA"

Plate 329

Esmond Mixing Bowl: (Pear pattern)
4" high, 6" diameter
Marked "OVEN WARE USA"

Note: This bowl was one of a nesting set.

Plate 330

#36 Esmond Shaded
Black/Brown Bean Pot:
8" high, 10" wide
Marked "ESMOND 36 USA"

Esmond Shaded
Black/Brown Individual
Bean Servers:
2¼" high, 3½" diameter
Marked "OVEN WARE USA"

132

Plate 331

Plate 332

Peedeeco Stick-Handled Casserole:
4" high, 11½" long
Marked "OVEN WARE PEEDEECO USA"

#17 Esmond Shaded Black/Brown
Ice-Lip Pitcher:
8" high, 8½" wide
Marked "ESMOND 17 USA"

Plate 333

Peedeeco Bean Pot Set:
Covered bean pot –
6¾" high, 8" wide
Marked "OVEN WARE
PEEDEECO USA"

Individual Servers –
2¼" high, 3½" diameter
No bottom mark

Plate 334

Peedeeco Stick-Handled
Individual Casserole:
3¾" high, 7½" long
Marked "OVEN WARE PEEDEECO USA"

CHAPTER THIRTEEN

Unusual and One-Of-A-Kind Items

In the fifteen years that the Watt Pottery Company produced hand-decorated kitchen ware, many different shapes, sizes, colors and patterns were created. Many lines were produced abundantly while others were extremely limited. However, there are many unique and distinctive pieces, examples of which are illustrated in this chapter, which were either experimental or specially made for a particular occasion or person. These rare, sometimes one-of-a-kind treasures are the most coveted by many Watt collectors and to them are considered invaluable and definitely irreplaceable. Rarity alone, however, is not the only factor to be considered. The value of these unusual pieces of Watt pottery is influenced by beauty, individuality, and eye appeal.

Plate 335

Rosebud Divided Dinner Plate:
(Experimental Piece)
10½" diameter
No bottom mark

Plate 336

#98 Green Ivy Covered Sugar:
4½" high, 5" wide, 3¼"
diameter at opening
Marked "98 USA"

#62 Green Ivy Creamer:
4¼" high, 4½" wide
Marked "62"
(Experimental Pieces)

Plate 337

Green Ivy Hourglass Salt and Pepper:
(Experimental Pieces)
4½" high, 2½" diameter
No bottom marks

135

Red Flower Salt and Pepper:
(Experimental Pieces)
4" high, 2½" diameter
No bottom marks
Note: This pattern was probably an experimental one for the red Starflower. Notice that the flower centers are yellow and green, there are six petals instead of four or five and there are veins in the leaves.

Plate 338

Plate 339

#62 Christmas Creamer:
On back is stenciled:
    Merry Christmas
       1957
    The Watt Pottery Co.
4¼" high, 4½" wide
Marked "62"
Extremely rare

Plate 340

#75 Christmas Individual Bean Server:
On back is stenciled:
    Merry Christmas
       1957
    The Watt Pottery Co.
2¼" high, 3½" wide
Marked "OVEN WARE 75 USA"
Extremely rare

Plate 341

"A Child's Grace" Dinner Plate:
10" diameter
Marked "WATT USA"
Note: This plate was specially ordered and is
extremely rare.

Plate 342

"Max" and "Marla" Mugs:
3½" high, 3½" diameter
Marked "ESMOND 31 USA"
Note: These Esmond mugs were specially painted for twins named
Max and Marla, and are probably one of a kind.

Plate 343

#72 Red Raised Bird Canister:
7" high, 7" diameter
Marked "WATT OVEN WARE 92 USA"
Note: Little information known on this
unusual piece. Probably had a lid – could
have been an experimental piece.

Plate 344

Watt Christmas Punch Bowl and Underplate:
This beautiful set is probably the most exquisite and unusual piece of Watt pottery
known to exist today. It was specially made for use at the Watt Christmas party in
1957. It is truly a most desirable and valuable piece of Watt pottery.
Punch Bowl:
7" high, 14" diameter
Marked "GOLD-N-BAKE WATT WARE OVEN WARE USA"
Underplate:
15" diameter
Marked "31 USA"

Plate 345

Mexican Bowl:
(Probably an experimental piece, decorated with red sombreros, green cactus, and yellow sun.)
2" high, 5½" diameter
Marked "OVEN WARE 74 USA"

Plate 346

Policeman Cookie Jar:
11" high, 7½" diameter
No bottom mark

Note: This cookie jar was one of a very limited experimental line. Although several were made, we are told that less than ten exist today. Not your typical Watt pottery.

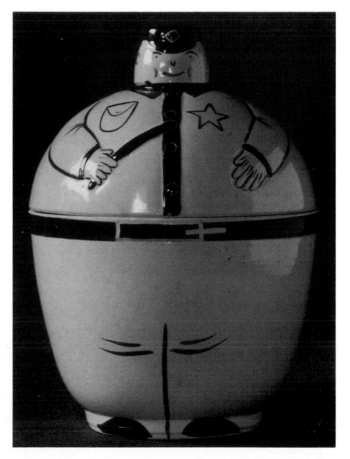

Plate 347

THIS IS A SAMPLE
ADVERTISING IMPRINT
THE WATT POTTERY CO.
CROOKSVILLE, OHIO

Advertising Ash Tray. (Salesman's sample)
Ad States:

"THIS IS A SAMPLE
ADVERTISING IMPRINT
THE WATT POTTERY CO.
CROOKSVILLE, OHIO"
4" diameter
No bottom mark
Rare

Apple Bowl – Factory Mistake
2¾" high, 11" diameter
Marked "OVEN WARE 611W USA"
Note: This mold was intended to be a
Woodgrain piece, but was painted with an
apple instead.

Plate 348

Plate 349

#15 Green/Red/Brown-Lined Pitcher:
(Experimental Piece)
5½" high, 5¾" wide
Marked "OVEN WARE 15 USA"

Plate 350

#8 Apple Bowl Trimmed In Gold
4¼" high, 8" diameter
Marked "WATT 8 OVEN WARE"
Note: This very unusual piece
has leaves outlined in bright gold
paint, and just a gold outline of a
leaf on the back side – could be
an experimental piece.

#15 White Design on Brown Pitcher:
(Experimental piece)
5½" high, 5¾" wide
Marked "WATT 15 MADE IN USA"

Plate 352

Plate 351

#49 Green/Red Lined Plate:
(Experimental piece)
12" diameter
Marked "WATT 49 USA"

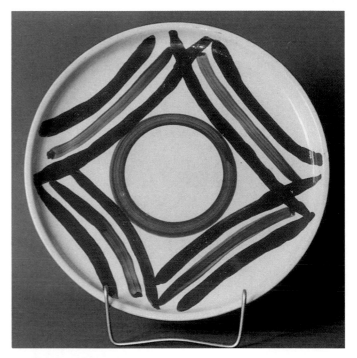

Plate 353

#49 Green/Red Leaves Plate:
(Experimental piece – artist signed
on back by "Mona")
12" diameter
Marked "WATT 49 USA"

Note: For a photograph of the bottom markings
on this plate see page 149.

141

Plate 354

Dark Blue/Red Sponged Hourglass Salt
and Pepper Set:
(Experimental pieces)
4½" high, 2½" diameter
No bottom marks

Plate 355

Lt. Blue Hourglass Salt and Pepper Set:
(Experimental pieces)
4½" high, 2½" diameter
No bottom marks

Shaded Brown Wall Pocket:
(Experimental piece)
3½" deep, 9" diameter
No bottom mark

Plate 357

Plate 356

Moon/Stars Brown Bowl:
2¾" high, 4¾" diameter
Silver sticker on bottom states:
"WATT WARE CROOKSVILLE, OHIO"
Note: There is no additional information
about this very unusual bowl. It has a
lined pattern with small moons and
stars surrounding the piece.

CHAPTER 14

Company Markings On Watt Pottery

The system used by the Watt Pottery Company to mark their pottery has been somewhat of a puzzle. The marks varied over the years but, because of lack of uniformity, it is difficult to date pieces by their bottom marks.

Most Watt ware is identified by an unmistakable, usually circular impression on the bottom of each piece. Each mold had a corresponding number which usually appeared on the bottom center of each piece. Certain pieces were typically unmarked, such as ice buckets, rectangular baking dishes, salt and pepper shakers, 9½" dinner plates and divided dinner plates.

Earlier "Pansy" pieces were simply marked "Watt" or "Watt U.S.A." and used a cursive style of lettering. A few pieces were marked "Eve-N-Bake Watt Ware Oven Ware U.S.A." with a large "W" logo. (The later "Eve-N-Bake" mark did not have the large "W" logo.) Although many of the early banded pieces were numbered, "Pansy" pieces were usually unnumbered. After production of the Starflower and Apple patterns began, block lettering was predominant in the bottom markings and most pieces were numbered. Most common markings were "Watt Oven Ware U.S.A.," "Oven Ware U.S.A.," or "Eve-N-Bake Oven Ware U.S.A." (without the "W" logo.) Many small pieces were simply marked with the mold number because of lack of space. In very rare cases a round foil sticker bearing the Watt Eagle logo was attached to the bottom of a piece. A similar, smaller sticker has been found on the top or inside of the pottery wares.

Because the Watts produced so many lines of pottery for other companies, these pieces bear either the company name or product line on the bottom. The "R-F Spaghetti" mark represents the Ravarino & Freschi, Inc. line of spaghetti ware. "Esmond," "Peedeeco," "Orchard Ware," "Cabinart," and "Heirloom" are other examples of this type of mark.

The "Kla Ham'rd" and "Kathy Kale" lines were special in that the pieces bore a mark labeling the series itself. Examples of these marks will appear in the pages that follow.

Certain lines such as the Woodgrain, Kla Ham'rd and Morning Glory series had their own individual numbering systems. Examples of these pieces, along with their corresponding mold numbers, appear in Chapter 12 on Miscellaneous Watt Ware.

Listed below are some of the most popular molds produced by the Watts with their corresponding number. It is not a complete listing, but does contain most of the pieces that are still found today. Keep in mind that these molds were not offered in all patterns and that there were a few exceptions to this general list.

#01 – Grease Jar, Covered 5½" high
#02 – 3 Pc. Refrigerator Set
#3/19 – Casserole, Covered 8½" diameter
#04 – Ribbed Bowl 4" diameter ⎤
#05 – Ribbed Bowl 5" diameter ⎬ nesting set
#06 – Ribbed Bowl 6" diameter
#07 – Ribbed Bowl 7" diameter ⎦
 #5 – Mixing Bowl (Ribbed/Unribbed) 5" diameter ⎤
 #6 – Mixing Bowl (Ribbed/Unribbed) 6" diameter
 #7 – Mixing Bowl (Ribbed/Unribbed) 7" diameter ⎬ nesting set
 #8 – Mixing Bowl (Ribbed/Unribbed) 8" diameter
 #9 – Mixing Bowl (Ribbed/Unribbed) 9" diameter ⎦
#10 – Mixing Bowl 10" diameter ⎤
#12 – Mixing Bowl 12" diameter ⎬ nesting set
#14 – Mixing Bowl 14" diameter ⎦
#15 – Pitcher 5½" high
#16 – Pitcher 6¾" high
#17 – Pitcher (With or Without Ice-Lip) 8" high
#18 – Tab-Handled Individual Casserole 5" diameter
#18 – Stick-Handled Individual Casserole 7½" long
#18 – French-Handled Individual Casserole 8" long
#21 – Cookie Jar 7½" high
#23 – Individual Salad or Cereal Bowl 5¾" diameter
#31 – Platter 15" diameter
#33 – Pie Plate 9" diameter
#39 – Spaghetti Bowl 13" diameter
#44 – Individual Spaghetti Bowl 8" diameter
#47 – Grease Jar, Covered 4½" high
#49 – Platter 12" diameter
#52 – Individual Salad or Cereal Bowl 6½" diameter
#53 – Bowl 7½" diameter
#54 – Bowl/Casserole, Covered 8½" diameter
#55 – Bowl 11¾" diameter
#56 – Tumbler 4" or 4½" high
#58 – Bowl 10½" diameter
#59 – Goodies Jar 8½" high
#61 – Mug 3" high
#62 – Creamer 4¼" high
#63 – Bowl 6½" diameter ⎤
#64 – Bowl 7½" diameter ⎬ nesting set
#65 – Bowl 8½" diameter ⎦

#66 – Bowl, Covered 7½" diameter

#67 – Bowl, Covered 8½" diameter

#68 – Individual Salad or Cereal Bowl 5" diameter

#69 – Refrigerator Pitcher (Square-Shaped) 8½" high

#72 – Large Canister/Goodies Jar 9½" high

#73 – Covered Casserole/Large Salad Bowl 9½" diameter

#74 – Individual Salad or Cereal Bowl 5½" diameter

#75 – Individual Bean Server 3½" diameter

#76 – Two-Handled Bean Pot 6½" high

#77 – Bowl, 7" diameter

#80 – Cheese Crock, Covered 8½" diameter

#81 – Canisters (Flour and Sugar), Covered 8" high

#82 – Canisters (Tea and Coffee), Covered 7" high

#86 – Oval Casserole, Covered 10" diameter

#91 – Dome Top Canister 10¾" high

#94 – Individual Salad or Cereal Bowl 6" diameter

#96 – Covered Baker 8½" diameter

#98 – Sugar, Covered 4½" high

#101 – Dinner Plate, 10" diameter

#102 – Salad Plate, 7½" diameter

#106 – Bowl, 10¾" diameter

#110/120 – Chip 'n Dip Set (#110 – 8" diameter, #120 – 5" diameter)

#112 – Teapot (standard spout) 6" high

#115 – Coffee Pot 9¾" high

#119 – Bowl 9" diameter

#121 – Mug 3¾" high

#126 – Oil/Vinegar Set 7" high

#131 – Covered Bowl 9" diameter

#501 – Mug 4½" high

#503 – Cookie Jar 8¼" high

#505 – Teapot (extended spout), 5¾" high

#600 – Ribbed Bowl, Covered 7¾" diameter ⎫ can also be used without
#601 – Ribbed Bowl, Covered 8¾" diameter ⎭ lids for nesting set #600-604

#602 – Ribbed Bowl 4¾" diameter

#603 – Ribbed Bowl 5¾" diameter

#604 – Ribbed Bowl 6¾" diameter

#701 – Mug 3¾" high

Some Examples of Common
Watt Pottery Company Markings

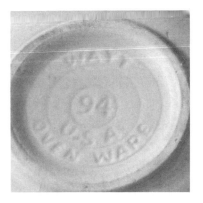

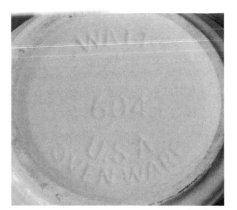

147

Watt Pottery bearing these marks was made
for the Ravarino & Freschi Company Inc.

Unusual foil sticker states:
"Watt – Crooksville, Ohio"
with an Eagle logo

Examples of the
"Orchard Ware" marking –
a special line of Watt
Pottery

Markings used for the "Kathy Kale" line

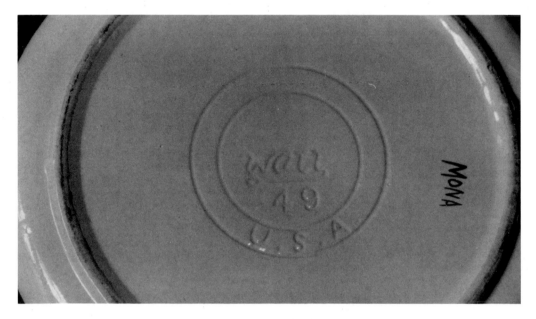

A very rare artist-signed platter by "Mona"

Example of the "Kla-Ham'rd" mark

The very unusual "Cabinart" mark was used on pottery made by Watt and sold by George Borgfeldt, Inc.

Watt

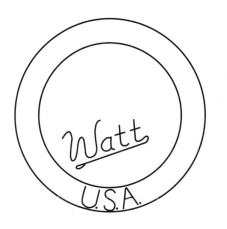

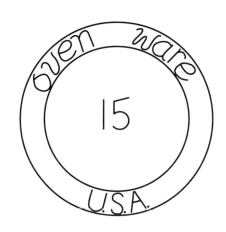

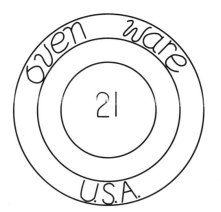

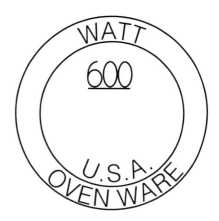

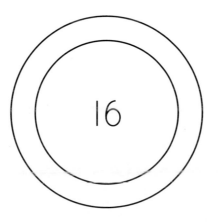

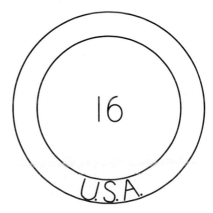

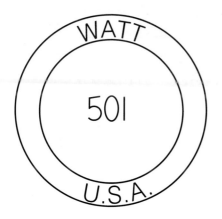

WATT
501
U.S.A.

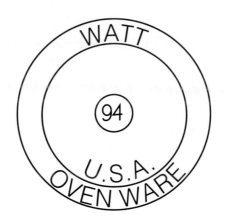

WATT
94
U.S.A.
OVEN WARE

WATT
7
U.S.A.
OVEN WARE

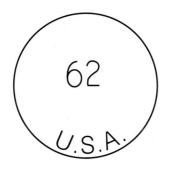

62
U.S.A.

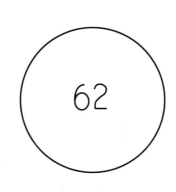

62

WATT
701
U.S.A.

WATT
604
U.S.A.
OVEN WARE

WATT
76
U.S.A.
OVEN WARE

WATT
112
U.S.A.
ORCHARD WARE

OVEN WARE
KLA
HAM'RD
43-19
MADE IN U.S.A.

OVEN WARE
U.S.A.
Peedeeco

31
ESMOND
U.S.A.

(CABINART)
U.S.A.
BAKE WARE

HEIRLOOM
306
U.S.A.

HEIRLOOM
STANDARD
810

KATHY KALE
U.S.A.

OVEN WARE
BAK ING
KITCHEN WARE

VALUE GUIDE

Although there is no definite value for any collectible, this price guide is intended to help the collector/dealer determine an approximate measure of value for a particular piece. The prices listed in this guide reflect the input of many collectors and dealers. However, because of the wide variety and uniqueness of Watt ware, what appeals to one collector may not appeal to another, so personal preference must be considered in determining the value of a particular piece. In many instances availability of a particular piece in a particular geographic location can affect the price, so it is advisable for a new collector to compare prices at shops and shows in his area to make a final determination of value. Communicating with other collectors is also a valuable tool in determining availability and value.

Although there are hundreds of pieces identified in this guide, new pieces are constantly being discovered which only adds to the fun of collecting this interesting pottery. Some collectors will try to find all the patterns of a particular item, such as #62 creamers (see bottom of page 5), while others will try to collect as many pieces of a particular pattern that they can locate. Still other collectors search for unusual pieces and are always on the prowl for a piece they have never seen before. To Watt collectors it is like a treasure hunt, and when they walk into a crowded antique shop or show, that colorful apple or crowing rooster will catch their eye from across the room.

The values in this guide assume that the piece is in mint condition, even though the photographed item is not. In some instances, bottom marks can vary slightly on pieces described. Dimensions given are approximations and widths, heights, or diameters listed are measured at the widest or highest point, unless otherwise noted. Please note that measurements may vary slightly due to factory run inconsistencies.

Some controversy exists as to whether advertising should add value to a piece. Although many collectors seek out pieces with clever advertising slogans or a certain town, other collectors rather collect pieces without advertising. This is merely a case of personal preference, and values in this book will not reflect the presence of advertising, but rather rarity and demand.

No prices available for items shown on pages 5–10, 30, 57, 74, 90, 96, 103, and 134.

PLATE	ITEM	PRICE	PLATE	ITEM	PRICE
1	Blue/White Banded Casserole	$45.00		Lt. Blue/White Banded Mixing Bowl	
	Blue/White Banded Pitcher	$95.00		(back)	$35.00
	Blue/White Banded			Lt. Blue/White Banded Pitcher	$95.00
	Mixing Bowls (each)	$25.00		Lt. Blue/White Banded Mixing Bowl	
2	Green/White			(front)	$25.00
	Banded Bowls (each)	$25.00	6	#17 Kitch-N-Queen Ice-Lip Pitcher	$200.00
3	White-Banded Covered Casserole	$55.00	7	Kitch-N-Queen Hourglass S/P (pair)	$225.00
4	White-Banded Pitcher	$85.00	8	Kitch-N-Queen Ribbed Mixing Bowls	
	White-Banded Bowl (front)	$25.00		#9	$50.00
	White-Banded Bowl (back)	$25.00		#8	$40.00
5	Lt. Blue/White Banded Cookie Jar	$100.00		#7 (not pictured)	$40.00

PLATE	ITEM	PRICE
	#6	$40.00
	#5	$45.00
9	#503 Kitch-N-Queen Cookie Jar	$225.00
10	Kitch-N-Queen Mixing Bowls:	
	#5 (pictured)	$45.00
	#6	$40.00
	#7	$40.00
	#8	$40.00
	#9	$50.00
	#10	$50.00
	#12	$60.00
	#14 (pictured)	$60.00
11	Raised Pansy French-Handled Individual Casserole	$90.00
12	Raised Pansy Pitcher	$225.00
13	Raised Pansy Refrigerator Pitcher w/lid	$100.00
14	Cut-Leaf Pansy Sugar & Creamer...pr)	$175.00
15	Cut-Leaf Pansy Dutch Oven	$175.00
16	Cut-Leaf Pansy Individ. Spaghetti Plate	$40.00
17	Cut-Leaf Pansy Platter	$110.00
18	Cut-Leaf Pansy Cup & Saucer	$90.00
19	Cut-Leaf Pansy Pitcher	$175.00
20	Cut-Leaf Pansy Pie Plate	$150.00
21	Cut-Leaf Pansy Mixing Bowls .....(each)	$45.00
22	Cut-Leaf Pansy Spaghetti Bowl	$80.00
23	Cut-Leaf Pansy Stick-Handled Individual Casserole	$125.00
24	Cut-Leaf Pansy Indiv. Serv. Bowls ...(ea)	$30.00
25	Cut-Leaf Pansy Individual Spaghetti Bowl	$35.00
26	Cut-Leaf Pansy Serving Bowls Bullseye Pattern 15"	$100.00
	Bullseye Pattern w/Red Swirls 11"	$90.00
27	Cut-Leaf Pansy Individual Serving Bowl	$35.00
28	Cut-Leaf Pansy Plate	$55.00
29	Cut-Leaf Pansy Saucer	$20.00
30	Cut-Leaf Pansy Platter	$110.00
31	Cut-Leaf Pansy Snack Set ....(set)	$150.00
32	Old Pansy Casserole	$75.00
	Cut-Leaf Pansy Casserole	$75.00
33	#8 Old Pansy Four-Handled Casserole	$90.00
34	#3/19 Old Pansy Casserole	$75.00
35	#39 Old Pansy Spaghetti Bowl	$80.00
36	#39 Old Pansy Spaghetti Bowl	$80.00
37	Old Pansy Indiv. Spaghetti Bowls (ea.)	$35.00
38	#49 Old Pansy Platter	$85.00
39	#31 Old Pansy Platter	$100.00
40	#15 Old Pansy Pitcher	$225.00
41	#17 Old Pansy Pitcher	$225.00
42	Old Pansy (Cross Hatch) Pitcher	$275.00
43	Old Pansy (Cross Hatch) Cookie Jar	$275.00
44	Old Pansy (Cross Hatch) Spaghetti Bowl	$250.00
45	Old Pansy (Cross Hatch) Platter	$175.00
46	#98 Apple Covered Sugar ....(w/lid)	$400.00
	(w/out lid)	$200.00
	#62 Apple Creamer	$90.00

PLATE	ITEM	PRICE
47	Apple Hourglass S/P, raised letters .(pair)	$275.00
	Apple Barrel-Shaped S/P ....(pair)	$600.00
	Apple Hourglass S/P ....(pair)	$250.00
48	#30 Apple Tumbler	$1,000.00
49	Apple Mugs	PRICED BELOW
50	#121 Apple Mug ....(each)	$185.00
51	#61 Apple Mug ....(each)	$500.00
52	#701 Apple Mug ....(each)	$500.00
53	#501 Apple Mug ....(each)	$350.00
54	Apple Dinner Plate 9½"	$450.00
	#101 Apple Dinner Plate 10"	$600.00
55	#31 Apple Platter 15"	$350.00
	#49 Apple Platter 12"	$400.00
56	(left to right):	
	#62 Apple Creamer	$90.00
	#15 Apple Pitcher	$75.00
	#16 Apple Pitcher	$110.00
	#17 Apple Pitcher	$275.00
57	(left to right):	
	#17 Apple Pitcher (no ice-lip)	$300.00
	#17 Apple Ice-Lip Pitcher	$275.00
	#69 Apple Refrigerator Pitcher (square-shaped)	$550.00
58	Apple Divided Plate	$2,000.00
59	Apple Divided Plate (small leaves) ....(each)	$2,000.00
60	Apple Tea Set	
	#505 Apple Teapot	$3,000.00
	Apple Creamer & Sugar ....(set)	$1,000.00
61	#112 Apple Teapot	$1,500.00
62	#115 Apple Coffee Pot	$3,000.00
63	#33 Apple Pie Plate	$150.00
64	#126 Apple Oil/Vinegar Set w/lids...................................(set)	$1,800.00
	w/out lids...............................(set)	$1,500.00
65	Apple Rectangular Baking Dish	$1,500.00
66	#52 Apple Cereal Bowl	$50.00
67	#94 Apple Cereal Bowls ....(each)	$50.00
68	#74 Apple Cereal Bowl	$45.00
69	#23 Apple Cereal Bowl	$75.00
70	#44 Apple Individual Spaghetti Bowl	$400.00
71	Apple Oval Bowl	$200.00
72	#106 Apple Bowl	$350.00
73	Apple Chip N' Dip Set (#120/#110) ..(set)	$300.00
74	Apple Ribbed Bowls (left to right)	
	#602	$125.00
	#603	$100.00
	#604	$90.00
75	Apple Ribbed Mixing Bowls (left to right)	
	#9 (not pictured)	$85.00
	#8	$55.00
	#7	$55.00
	#6	$55.00
	#5	$65.00
76	Apple Mixing Bowls (largest to smallest)	
	#9	$85.00
	#8	$45.00

PLATE	ITEM	PRICE
	#7	$45.00
	#6	$45.00
	#5	$55.00
77	Apple Mixing Bowls (left to right)	
	#65	$90.00
	#64	$60.00
	#63	$50.00
78	Apple Ribbed Mixing Bowls (left to right)	
	#04	$65.00
	#05	$60.00
	#06	$50.00
	#07	$50.00
79	#39 Apple Spaghetti Bowl	$175.00
80	#73 Apple Bowl (left)	$85.00
	#55 Apple Bowl (right)	$250.00
81	#18 Apple French-Handled Individual Casserole	$225.00
82	#18 Apple Stick-Handled Individual Casserole (left)	$175.00
	#18 Apple French-Handled Individual Casserole (right)	$225.00
83	Apple Fondue w/out lid	$900.00
84	#18 Tab-Handled Indiv. Casserole	$225.00
85	#05 Apple Covered Bowl, Ribbed	$145.00
86	#01 Apple Grease Jar	$375.00
87	#503 Apple Cookie Jar	$450.00
88	#21 Apple Cookie Jar	$475.00
89	#76 Apple Two-Handled Bean Pot	$175.00
	#75 Apple Individual Bean Server	$250.00
90	Apple Casserole Warmers (each)	$1,000.00
91	#131 Apple Covered Bowl	$175.00
92	#600 Apple Ribbed Covered Bowl (left)	$125.00
	#601 Apple Ribbed Covered Bowl (right)	$125.00
93	#96 Apple Covered Baker, Small Handle	$125.00
94	#96 Apple Covered Baker, Large Handle	$125.00
95	Apple Ice Bucket	$275.00
96	#80 Apple Cheese Crock	$1,500.00
97	#72 Large Apple Canister	$500.00
98	#91 Apple Dome-Top Canister	$900.00
99	#67 Apple Covered Bowl	$125.00
100	Apple Canister Set (set)	$2,000.00
101	#3/19 Apple Casserole on Stand	$265.00
102	#73 Apple Dutch Oven Casserole	$235.00
103	#62 Double Apple Creamer	$400.00
104	#96 Double Apple Covered Baker on Stand	$250.00
105	Reduced Decoration Apple Mixing Bowl (left)	$85.00
	Reduced Decoration Apple Mixing Bowl (right)	$90.00
106	Reduced Decoration Apple Lazy Susan Set (set)	$900.00
107	Double Apple Mixing Bowls	
	#04	$110.00
	#05	$90.00
	#06	$75.00
	#07	$75.00
108	#73 Double Apple Bowl	$125.00
109	Open Apple Mixing Bowls (largest to smallest)	
	#8	$175.00
	#7	$150.00
	#6	$150.00
	#5	$175.00
110	#76 Starflower Two-Handled Bean Pot	$175.00
	#75 Starflower Indiv. Bean Servers (each)	$50.00
111	#47 Starflower Grease Jar	$250.00
112	#56 Starflower Tumblers	
	Round-Sided Tumbler	$275.00
	Slant-Sided Tumbler	$325.00
113	Starflower Mugs	
	#121 Starflower Mug (left)	$275.00
	#501 Starflower Mug (right)	$100.00
114	Starflower Salt & Pepper Sets	
	Barrel-Shaped S/P (left) (pair)	$375.00
	Hourglass S/P (center) (pair)	$275.00
	Barrel-Shaped S/P (right) (pair)	$175.00
115	#18 Starflower Stick-Handled Individual Casserole	$125.00
116	Starflower Ice Bucket	$185.00
117	#18 Starflower French-Handled Individual Casserole	$200.00
118	#18 Starflower Tab-Handled Individual Casserole	$125.00
119	Starflower Creamer & Pitchers (left to right)	
	#62 Starflower Creamer	$250.00
	#15 Starflower Pitcher	$65.00
	#16 Starflower Pitcher	$85.00
	#17 Starflower Ice-Lip Pitcher	$175.00
120	#17 Starflower Ice-Lip Pitcher (four petal)	$225.00
121	#69 Starflower Refrigerator Pitcher	$700.00
122	Starflower Berry Bowls (each)	$35.00
123	#74 Starflower Cereal Bowl	$25.00
124	#64 Starflower Bowl	$50.00
125	#73 Starflower Bowl	$65.00
126	#39 Starflower Bowl	$110.00
127	#33 Starflower Pie Plate	$200.00
128	#31 Starflower Platter	$110.00
129	#54 Starflower Covered Casserole	$125.00
130	#21 Starflower Cookie Jar	$185.00
131	#96 Starflower Covered Baker On Warming Stand	$150.00
132	Starflower Mixing Bowls (left to right)	
	#5	$60.00
	#6 (pictured)	$45.00
	#7 (pictured)	$45.00
	#8 (pictured)	$45.00
	#9	$55.00

PLATE	ITEM	PRICE
133	Starflower Bowls (left to right)	
	#52 Cereal/Salad Bowl	$30.00
	#53	$40.00
	#54	$45.00
134	Starflower Mixing Bowls (left to right)	
	#04	$65.00
	#05	$50.00
	#06	$45.00
	#07 (not pictured)	$45.00
135	#56 Green-On-Brown Starflower Tumbler	$175.00
	#17 Green-On-Brown Starflower Pitcher	$175.00
136	#5 Green-On-Brown Starflower Mixing Bowl	$35.00
137	#15 Green-On-Brown Starflower Pitcher (left)	$190.00
	#18 Green-On-Brown Starflower Tab-Handled Individual Casserole (center)	$45.00
	#16 Green-On-Brown Starflower Pitcher (right)	$110.00
138	#39 Green-On-Brown Starflower Spaghetti Bowl	$90.00
139	#54 Green-On-Brown Starflower Covered Casserole	$90.00
140	#21 Green-On-Brown Starflower Cookie Jar	$125.00
141	#31 Green-On-Brown Starflower Platter	$90.00
142	Pink-On Green Starflower Bread Plate	$35.00
143	Pink-On-Green Starflower Dinner Plate	$100.00
144	Pink-On-Green Starflower Berry Bowls	(each) $35.00
145	Pink-On-Green Starflower Cup & Saucer	$65.00
146	Pink-On-Green Starflower Berry Set On Spinning Wood Base	(set) $350.00
147	Pink-On-Green Starflower Stick-Handled Individual Casserole	$125.00
148	#31 Pink-On-Green Starflower Platter	$110.00
149	Pink-On-Green Starflower Covered Casserole	$125.00
150	White-On-Green Starflower Bowl	$100.00
151	Pink-On-Black Starflower Stick-Handled Individual Casserole	$150.00
152	Pink-On-Black Berry Bowls	(each) 45.00
153	Pink-On-Black Starflower Covered Casserole	$125.00
154	Pink-On-Black Starflower Bowl	$125.00
155	Pink-On-Black Starflower Cup & Saucer	$85.00
156	Pink-On-Black Sugar	$75.00
157	#39 White-On-Red Starflower Spaghetti Bowl	$190.00
158	#121 White-On-Red Starflower Mug	$400.00
159	#39 White-On-Blue Starflower Spaghetti Bowl	$250.00
160	#15 Tulip Pitcher	$550.00
161	#62 Tulip Creamer (front)	$225.00

PLATE	ITEM	PRICE
	#16 Tulip Pitcher (back left)	$175.00
	#17 Tulip Ice-Lip Pitcher (back right)	$300.00
162	Tulip Mixing Bowls (left to right)	
	#63	$75.00
	#64	$85.00
	#65	$110.00
163	#603 Tulip Mixing Bowls	
	#600	$125.00
	#601	$125.00
	#602	$275.00
	#603 (pictured)	$250.00
	#604	$150.00
164	#600 Tulip Ribbed Covered Bowl	$250.00
165	#73 Tulip Bowl	$150.00
166	#503 Tulip Cookie Jar	$375.00
167	Dutch Tulip Divided Plate	$800.00
168	#62 Dutch Tulip Creamer (left)	$275.00
	#15 Dutch Tulip Pitcher (center)	$250.00
	#16 Dutch Tulip Pitcher (right)	$250.00
169	#69 Dutch Tulip Refrigerator Pitcher	$600.00
170	#18 Dutch Tulip French-Handled Individual Casserole	$275.00
171	#05 Dutch Tulip Covered Bowl	$250.00
172	Dutch Tulip Mixing Bowls (left to right)	
	#63	$100.00
	#64	$110.00
	#65	$150.00
173	Dutch Tulip Bowls	
	#5	$150.00
	#6 (pictured)	$100.00
	#7	$100.00
	#8	$110.00
	#9	$140.00
174	Dutch Tulip Serving Set	$550.00
175	#67 Dutch Tulip Covered Bowl	$250.00
176	#76 Dutch Tulip Two-Handled Bean Pot	$350.00
177	#80 Dutch Tulip Cheese Crock	$475.00
178	#39 Dutch Tulip Spaghetti Bowl	$400.00
179	Dutch Tulip Canister Set (set of 4)	$2,500.00
180	#15 Cherry Pitcher (Salesman's sample)	$200.00
181	#15 Cherry Pitcher (left)	$175.00
	#17 Cherry Pitcher (right)	$275.00
182	#21 Cherry Cookie Jar	$275.00
183	#3/19 Cherry Covered Casserole	$175.00
184	#39 Cherry Spaghetti Bowl	$150.00
185	#31 Cherry Platter	$145.00
186	#23 Cherry Cereal Bowl	$50.00
187	Cherry Mixing Bowls	
	#6 (left)	$40.00
	#8 (right)	$45.00
188	#4 Cherry Berry Bowl	$45.00
189	#52 Cherry Cereal Bowls	(each) $45.00
190	Cherry Barrel-Shaped Salt Shaker	$90.00
191	Tear Drop Serving Set	
	#73 Tear Drop Bowl	$130.00
	#74 Tear Drop Bowls	(each) $35.00

PLATE	ITEM	PRICE
192	#62 Tear Drop Creamer (left)	$275.00
	#15 Tear Drop Pitcher (center)	$60.00
	#16 Tear Drop Pitcher (right)	$150.00
193	#69 Tear Drop Refrigerator Pitcher	$500.00
194	Tear Drop Barrel-Shaped S/P	(pair) $350.00
195	#18 Tear Drop French-Handled Individual Casserole	$250.00
196	#76 Tear Drop Two-Handled Bean Pot	$110.00
	#75 Tear Drop Individual Bean Serv.	(ea) $30.00
197	Tear Drop Square-Shaped Covered Casserole	$850.00
198	#80 Tear Drop Cheese Crock	$375.00
199	#86 Tear Drop Covered Casserole	$750.00
200	#66 Tear Drop Bowl	$45.00
201	Tear Drop Mixing Bowls (left to right)	
	#5	$65.00
	#6 (pictured)	$45.00
	#7 (pictured)	$45.00
	#8	$45.00
	#9	$55.00
202	Tear Drop Mixing Bowls (left to right)	
	#04	$55.00
	#05 (pictured)	$45.00
	#06	$40.00
	#07 (pictured)	$40.00
203	Tear Drop Mixing Bowls (left to right)	
	#63	$45.00
	#64	$50.00
	#65	$55.00
204	#69 Rooster Refrigerator Pitcher	$550.00
205	#15 Rooster Pitcher (left)	$145.00
	#16 Rooster Pitcher (right)	$165.00
206	#05 Rooster Covered Bowl	$190.00
207	#18 Rooster French-Handled Individual Casserole	$245.00
208	Rooster Hourglass S/P (left)	(pr) $400.00
	Rooster Barrel-Shaped S/P (right)	(pr) $400.00
209	#98 Rooster Covered Sugar w/lid	$500.00
	w/out lid	$200.00
	#62 Rooster Creamer	$250.00
210	Rooster Canister Set (set of 4)	$2,800.00
211	#76 Rooster Two-Handled Bean Pot	$350.00
212	Rooster Ice Bucket	$275.00
213	#67 Rooster Covered Bowl	$200.00
214	Rooster Nesting Bowls	
	#68	$115.00
	#60	$100.00
	#67	000.00
215	Rooster Mixing Bowls (left to right)	
	#5 (pictured)	$85.00
	#6	$65.00
	#7	$65.00
	#8	$65.00
	#9	$100.00
	#63 (pictured)	$85.00
	#64	$95.00
	#65	$110.00

PLATE	ITEM	PRICE
216	#73 Rooster Bowl	$145.00
217	#58 Rooster Bowl	$275.00
218	#67 Rooster Bowl (no lid)	$90.00
219	Rooster Rectangular Baking Dish	$1,000.00
220	Rooster #39 Spaghetti Bowl	$375.00
221	#98 Autumn Foliage Covered Sugar w/lid	$300.00
	w/out lid	$150.00
	#62 Autumn Foliage Creamer	$200.00
222	#126 Autumn Foliage Oil/Vinegar Set w/lids	(set) $550.00
	w/out lids	(set) $250.00
223	Autumn Foliage Hourglass Salt/Pepper (left)	(pair) $175.00
	Autumn Foliage Hourglass Salt/Pepper, raised letters, (right)	(pair) $190.00
224	#121 Autumn Foliage Mug (left)	$200.00
	#501 Autumn Foliage Mug (right)	$175.00
225	Autumn Foliage Fondue (w/lid)	$275.00
226	Autumn Foliage Ice Bucket	$200.00
227	#33 Autumn Foliage Pie Plate	$125.00
228	#31 Autumn Foliage Platter	$110.00
229	#96 Autumn Foliage Covered Baker	$90.00
230	#15 Autumn Foliage Pitcher (left)	$65.00
	#16 Autumn Foliage Pitcher (center)	$75.00
	#17 Autumn Foliage Ice-Lip Pitcher	$165.00
231	Autumn Foliage Ribbed Bowls	
	#5 (pictured)	$45.00
	#6, #7, #8	$40.00
	#9	$45.00
232	Autumn Foliage Ribbed Bowls	
	#600 (pictured), #601	$35.00
	#602, #603	$65.00
	#604	$55.00
233	Autumn Foliage Mixing Bowls (left to right)	
	#65 (pictured)	$50.00
	#64	$45.00
	#63 (pictured)	$40.00
234	#94 Autumn Foliage Cereal Bowl	$30.00
235	#73 Autumn Foliage Bowl	$85.00
236	#106 Autumn Foliage Bowl	$85.00
237	#505 Autumn Foliage Teapot	$1,600.00
238	#76 Autumn Foliage Two-Handled Bean Pot	$150.00
239	#02 Autumn Foliage Refrigerator Dish (one section of a two-stacker covered piece)	$165.00
240	#04 Yellow Morning Glory Casserole w/lid	$275.00
	w/out lid	$150.00
241	Yellow Morning Glory Mixing Bowls	
	#5	$150.00
	#6, #7 (both pictured), #8	$75.00
	#9	$90.00
242	#96 Morning Glory Ice-Lip Pitcher	$375.00
243	#98 Morning Glory Sugar	$250.00
	#97 Morning Glory Creamer	$500.00

PLATE	ITEM	PRICE
244	Morning Glory Mixing Bowls (largest to smallest)	
	#9	$100.00
	#8	$85.00
	#7	$85.00
	#6	$85.00
	#5 (not pictured)	$160.00
245	#95 Morning Glory Cookie Jar	$400.00
246	#72 Eagle Canister	$600.00
247	Eagle Ice-Lip Pitcher	$450.00
248	Eagle Mixing Bowls, Ribbed	
	#5	$150.00
	#6	$125.00
	#7 (pictured)	$125.00
	#8	$135.00
	#9	$145.00
249	Eagle Mixing Bowls (left to right)	
	#12	$145.00
	#10	$145.00
250	Eagle Cereal Bowl	$85.00
251	#73 Eagle Bowl	$135.00
252	Dogwood Bread Plate	$55.00
253	Dogwood Platter	$110.00
254	Dogwood Serving Bowl	$110.00
255	White Daisy Salad Plate	$65.00
256	White Daisy Pitcher	$165.00
257	White Daisy Cup & Saucer	$75.00
258	White Daisy Stick-Handled Individual Casserole	$125.00
259	White Daisy Covered Casserole	$145.00
260	White Daisy Mixing Bowls (smallest to largest)	
	#5	$85.00
	#6 (not pictured)	$55.00
	#7	$55.00
	#8	$55.00
	#9	$65.00
261	#7 Butterfly Bowl	$275.00
262	Butterfly Ice Bucket (w/lid)	$800.00
263	#98 Brown-Banded Covered Sugar	
	w/lid	$200.00
	w/out lid	$90.00
	#62 Brown-Banded Creamer	$300.00
264	#121 Brown-Banded Mug	$125.00
265	#112 Brown-Banded Teapot	$700.00
266	#115 Brown-Banded Coffee Pot	$850.00
267	#102 Brown-Banded Salad Plate (left)	$25.00
	#31 Brown-Banded Platter (right)	$100.00
268	Woodgrain Pitchers (left to right)	
	#613W	$75.00
	#614W	$75.00
	#615W	$100.00
269	#611W Woodgrain Chip 'N Dip Bowl	$75.00
270	#608W Woodgrain Covered Bowl	$65.00
271	#617W Woodgrain Cookie Barrel	$90.00
272	NOT WATT! None of the Kathy Kale ware in brown glaze with white drip edge was made by the Watt Pottery Company	N/A

PLATE	ITEM	PRICE
273	Kathy Kale Bowls (experimental glazes — most Watt-made Kathy Kale ware was glazed in pure white)	(each) $65.00
274	NOT WATT! This hand decorated Kathy Kale serving set was produced by the Nelson McCoy Company	N/A
275	Green/Brown Leaves Canister Set w/Wood Lids	$300.00
276	Snack Bowl Set	$400.00
277	#76 Goodies Jar	$275.00
278	#59 Goodies Jar	$350.00
279	#72 Goodies Jar	$350.00
280	Kla Ham'rd Stacking Refrigerator Jar	$40.00
281	Kla Ham'rd Bowl	$25.00
282	#43-13 Kla Ham'rd Pie Plate	$45.00
283	#43-14 Kla Ham'rd Pitcher	$55.00
	#43-1 Stick-Handled Individual Casserole	$35.00
284	#43-12 Kla Ham'rd Covered Casserole (left)	$50.00
	#43-19 Kla Ham'rd Covered Casserole (right)	$55.00
285	#43-18 Kla Ham'rd Two-Handled Casserole	$60.00
286	Multi-Colored Basketweave Bowls	(each) $30.00
287	Lt. Green Basketweave Bowl Set	$100.00
288	Brown Basketweave Covered Casseroles	
	(left)	$30.00
	(right)	$30.00
289	Brown Basketweave Two-Handled Beanpot	$40.00
290	Brown Basketweave (left to right)	
	#806 Mug	(each) $10.00
	#801 Mug	(each) $10.00
	#100 Bowl	(each) $5.00
	#814 Individual Server	(each) $10.00
	#810 Ice-Lip Pitcher	$55.00
291	#806 Heirloom Brown Basketweave Mugs w/Original Box (set of 3 in a box)	$35.00
292	Heirloom #806 Cream-Colored Basketweave Mug	$15.00
293	Multi-Color Swirl-Sided Bowls	(each) $30.00
294	#17 Green Swirl-Sided Pitcher	$90.00
	#21 Green Swirl-Sided Cookie Jar	$100.00
	#9 Green Swirl-Sided Bowl	$30.00
295	Multi-Color Panel-Sided Mixing Bowls (smallest to largest)	
	#7	$25.00
	#8	$25.00
	#10	$35.00
296	White Spray/Teal Green Casseroles	
	#54 Covered Casserole	$75.00
	#18 Tab-Handled Indiv. Casserole	$85.00
297	Speckled Watt Ware	
	#106 Salad Bowl	$25.00

PLATE	ITEM	PRICE
	#120 Bowl	$10.00
	Vinegar/Oil Set	(set) $100.00
	Hourglass S/P	(pair) $45.00
298	Brown Drip Glaze Bowls	(each) $35.00
299	#96 Brown/Cream Covered Bowl	$55.00
300	Cabinart Brown/Cream Covered Pitcher	$35.00
301	Lt. Green/Brown Creamer	$300.00
302	#62 Olive Green/Brown Creamer	$300.00
303	Lt. Green/Brown Pitcher	$55.00
304	Brown/Green and Brown/Blue Mixing Bowls	(each) $25.00
305	Brown Glaze Electric Warmer	$125.00
306	Brown Glaze Carafe	$175.00
307	Brown Glaze Beanpot	$25.00
308	#7 Brown Glazed Dog Dish	$75.00
309	Shaded Brown Mug	$10.00
310	Shaded Brown Casserole	$25.00
311	Shaded Brown Cookie Jar	$35.00
312	Shaded Brown Pitcher	$40.00
313	Shaded Brown Mixing Bowls	(each) $25.00
314	Shaded Brown Mixing Bowls	(each) $20.00
315	#603 Shaded Brown Mexican Bowl	$25.00
316	Iced Tea Dispenser	$125.00
317	Matte-Finish Tea Set	
	Teapot w/lid	$95.00
	Sugar	$55.00
	Creamer	$95.00
318	#76 Matte-Finish Two-Handled Bean Pot	$25.00
	#75 Matte-Finish Individual Bean Servers	(each) $10.00
319	#126 Matte-Finish Oil/Vinegar Set w/lids	$85.00
320	Matte-Finish Salt/Pepper	(set) $25.00
321	Matte-Finish Serving Set	(set) $50.00
322	Esmond Cookie Jar w/Wood Lid	$100.00
323	#36 Esmond Cookie Jar	$100.00
324	Esmond Two-Handled Bean Pot	$150.00
	Esmond Individual Bean Servers	(ea) $140.00
325	Esmond Platter	$175.00
326	Esmond 4-Section Canister Set on Wood Base w/Wood Lid	$125.00
327	NOT WATT! This special ripple glaze was probably made by the Nelson McCoy Co.	N/A

PLATE	ITEM	PRICE
328	#31 Esmond Grape Mug	$200.00
329	Esmond Mixing Bowl (pear pattern)	$75.00
330	#36 Esmond Shaded Black/Brown Bean Pot	$85.00
	Esmond Shaded Black/Brown Individual Bean Servers	(each) $15.00
331	#17 Esmond Shaded Black/Brown Ice-Lip Pitcher	$125.00
332	Peedeeco Stick-Handled Casserole	$50.00
333	Peedeeco Bean Pot Set	
	Covered Bean Pot	$45.00
	Individual Servers	(each) $5.00
334	Peedeeco Stick-Handled Individual Casserole	$25.00
335	Rosebud Divided Dinner Plate	$800.00–1,000.00+
336	#98 Green Ivy Covered Sugar w/lid	$700.00–900.00+
	#62 Green Ivy Creamer	$1,500.00+
337	Green Ivy Hourglass S/P	$700.00–900.00+
338	Red Flower Salt/Pepper	(pair) $400.00
339	#62 Christmas Creamer	$2,000.00+
340	#75 Christmas Individual Bean Server (used as sugar bowl)	$800.00+
341	"A Child's Grace" Dinner Plate	$600.00–800.00
342	"Max" and "Marla" Mugs	(set) $700.00–900.00+
343	#72 Red Raised Bird Canister	$800.00–1,000.00
344	Watt Christmas Punch Bowl and Underplate	$6,000.00+
345	Mexican Bowl	$85.00
346	Policeman Cookie Jar	$1,200.00+
347	Advertising Ash Tray	$150.00
348	Apple Bowl (factory mistake)	$250.00
349	#15 Green/Red/Brown-Lined Pitcher	$400.00+
350	#8 Apple Bowl Trimmed In Gold	$250.00
351	#15 White Design On Brown Pitcher	$400.00+
352	#49 Green/Red Lined Plate	$275.00
353	#49 Green/Red Leaves Plate	$400.00–500.00+
354	Dark Blue/Red Sponged Hourglass Salt & Pepper	(set) $250.00–300.00
355	Lt. Blue Hourglass Salt/Pepper	(pair) $200.00
356	NOT WATT! Although very similar to Watt's molds and colors, the authors hesitate to attribute this piece to Watt.	N/A
357	Moon/Stars Brown Bowl	$35.00